The Art of Choosing You Unapologetically

8 STEPS TO HAPPINESS, HEALTH, AND WELLNESS WORKBOOK

RENEE CAGE, LCSW

The Art of Choosing You Unapologetically ~ 8 Steps to Happiness, Health, and Wellness Workbook
Copyright © 2024 by Renee Cage, LCSW
ALL RIGHTS RESERVED

ISBN - 979-8-9914010-0-5

Cover Design by Stacey Debono
Edited by Stacey Debono

www.empoweredbycourage.com
www.reneespeakswellness.com
www.ichoosemebrand.com

Table of Contents

Foreword

In today's fast-paced world, filled with endless choices and competing priorities, it's easy for women to lose sight of themselves amidst the noise. In *The Art of Choosing You*, Renee Cage offers a compelling roadmap for women to reclaim their power, prioritize their well-being, and chart a course toward personal fulfillment. As someone deeply invested in the principles of emotional intelligence and personal growth, I am honored to introduce Rene's transformative work to you.

Through her insightful exploration of empowerment and growth, Renee masterfully weaves together practical wisdom, heartfelt anecdotes, and actionable strategies to guide readers on a journey of self-discovery and self-mastery. With each page, she empowers women to embrace their authenticity, honor their desires, and cultivate a deeper sense of self-awareness.

What sets *The Art of Choosing You* apart is Renee's genuine empathy and unwavering commitment to uplifting others. Her words resonate deeply, offering a beacon of hope and inspiration for women seeking to navigate life's challenges with grace and resilience. By encouraging readers to prioritize self-care and self-compassion, she invites them to embark on a transformative journey toward greater confidence, fulfillment, and joy.

As you embark on this empowering odyssey with Renee Cage, may you find solace in her wisdom, courage in her vulnerability, and strength in her words. For within these pages lies the blueprint for a life of authenticity, purpose, and profound self-love. It is my sincere belief that *The Art of Choosing You* will serve as a guiding light for women everywhere, empowering them to embrace their true essence and live a life of limitless possibility.

With heartfelt regards,

DB "The Ei Guy" Bedford

Dear Amara,

I dedicate this book to you. At 21, you are stepping into a world brimming with possibilities. May your journey be filled with courage, wisdom, and joy. I am incredibly proud of the person you've become, and I cherish every moment we've shared. Always remember to chase your dreams, never give up, believe in yourself, and choose yourself unapologetically, for you are capable of amazing things. You are my shining star, my guiding light, and my forever love and I am honored to be your mother.

With all my love,
Mom

Introduction

Many years ago, when I first worked with a life coach, I was given the task of writing my story. As overwhelming as I thought it would be to write and rehash my life, it actually became the start of this book. This book has been in my belly for over 15 years. I have had many starts and stops with this book and different ideas of how I would present this book to the world. This is not just a book; this is part of my life, my journey, my lessons, my pain, my love, my healing, and my transformation. Where I am now as a grown-ass woman is certainly not where I started. Sure, I am proud of my accomplishments. I'm also grateful for my painful lessons.

I had a 25+ year career in child welfare, moving up through the ranks. I have a thriving mental health private practice. I get to work with incredible women. I love coaching clients. I get to travel the world and inspire women. I have a beautiful family and friend circle that loves and supports me. I get to witness my daughter thriving and living her best life at an HBCU. I am healthy and enjoy activities like weight training, yoga, skating, dancing, shooting at the range, hiking, rowing, reading, and painting. I love music and going to live concerts. I most love going for morning walks, sipping my homemade ginger, lemon, and pineapple tea, and appreciating the sun shining on my face in the zen Shabana area I created in my backyard. I want to celebrate my wins louder than I cry about my losses. I want to focus more on the good than the bad.

In this journey, I have gained strategies and tools from trial and error in life. They are tools I have also learned through my work and professional development and training. For me, I appreciate tools and strategies to help guide me. I hope you will utilize the tools in this book to guide you to your most desired place, where you accept every part of you, even the parts you want to work on.

This is why I created the E.M.P.O.W.E.R. framework. I wanted to share with other women the core mindset shifts it requires to live the of your fullest potential all while having the freedom and balance you deserve.

The Art of Choosing You Unapologetically is a transformative self-help workbook designed for women who are ready to embrace their true potential and lead a life of purpose and fulfillment. Through the unique E.M.P.O.W.E.R. framework, readers are guided through a comprehensive journey of self-assessment, introspection, and actionable steps for personal growth. Each chapter is meticulously crafted to address crucial aspects of personal development, from identifying and overcoming limiting beliefs to nurturing self-compassion, cultivating mindfulness, and building meaningful relationships. This workbook not only empowers women to prioritize self-care but also equips them with the tools to rewrite their life narratives and embrace their passions with excitement. With practical exercises and insightful guidance, E.M.P.O.W.E.R. is a beacon of empowerment, encouraging women to embrace their inner strength and live authentically.

EMPOWER

CHAPTER 1

Getting Started - Setting Intentions

I invite you to take inventory of your life and question yourself. Who are you? What do you want? Who will you be? What will you do? What will you have? Then ask yourself, "Who am I now?" Don't ask, "Am I happy?" Happy is an attitude. Happy is a mindset. We'll do more exploration of the mindset in the next chapter, but for now, this is the opportunity for you to set your intentions and make your commitment to yourself and your happiness. This is a choice; this is your choice to make.

Here's the thing, when we are ready to see changes in our life, we have to do the work. No one is coming to make you do it. No one is coming to tell you to turn off the TV, no one is coming to tell you to get out to exercise, no one is coming to tell you to eat healthily, and no one is coming to tell you to heal parts of yourself. Nobody's coming to tell you to apply for that job that you've always dreamt about. Nobody's coming to write the business plan for you. It's up to *you*!

I'm at the stage in my life where I only desire the best for myself! My mental health is number one. I desire everything God said I can have. I am claiming it and seizing it. This is my attitude. I desire to travel the world. I desire to eat good food. I desire to try and experience new things and I desire nothing but positive vibrations, energy, and people around me. It's blocking and eliminating season, blocking and eliminating toxicity. Toxicity comes in the form of people, places, and things. Whatever that is in your life that is not serving you must go!

In addition to people, places, and things, we also must block and eliminate our negative thoughts and beliefs about ourselves. In the next chapter, we'll get more into that and how to shift and challenge those thoughts. But for now, are you ready? Do you know you are worthy of extreme joy and happiness? Are you prepared to do what it takes to have it? If you answered yes, then this book is for you. It's your time! It's your time to dig deep and uncover those parts of you that you have not tended to, those parts that you have shrunk, those parts you have betrayed, those parts that you must forgive, those parts you must embrace and love on. It's your time, Sis.

Start where you are. You are in the perfect place. I will be with you on this journey. In the next section, you'll take a closer look at your current status. Turn on your GPS so it can say "You are here". Don't worry, you won't get lost.

My intention in creating the E.M.P.O.W.E.R. framework was to support you in jump-starting your desire for growth so that you see real results in real-time. I hope that this workbook provides you with an understanding of some of your behaviors so that you can have compassion for yourself as you create the life and person you want to be while embracing and honoring who you are now with love and acceptance.

I have determined that I am a person with a multifaceted experience and there are several parts to me that must be nurtured. I have concluded that these parts are to be nurtured by me and that it is unrealistic to rely on anyone outside of me to do that for me. But life wasn't always so groovy. I have had plenty of bumps and bruises along the way. Notably, my start of life was extremely bumpy. My mother jumped out of a two-story window attempting to get away from my father and a vicious beating while seven months pregnant with me. My father was my mother's exploiter when she was a teen and her pimp as an adult. I was abandoned by my parents and experienced a gamut of life-altering traumatic events. When starting to dig deep and make changes, you gotta assess where you are and acknowledge where you've been. I had to start at the beginning to gain an understanding of myself. And that is where you must start.

Where Are You?

For E.M.P.O.W.E.R. to take you to the next level so that you are being the best version of yourself and living the best version of your life, you have to be real about where you are right now, in this moment. This is not to highlight what you think is wrong. It's to highlight what's working in your life, identify areas that you may want to grow in, and gain acceptance of some areas that will just be. My favorite exercise to get started on how we are doing in life is called the *Wheel of Life*. The Wheel of Life helps give you a visual of eight categories that represent areas of life.

Balance is one of the main complaints from the clients I work with, and it is unique to everyone. What one person may feel like an easy schedule to manage could feel like total chaos for another person. This exercise also helps you have better awareness and allows you to be intentional in making the life you dream, your best-balanced life.

This exercise is not a one-and-done. I recommend you do this periodically throughout your life. Why? Well, our outlook will shift over time. Our priorities change over time. Life is constantly transforming and so does our sense of balance and our focus on what's important. Now it's time to complete the Wheel of Life.

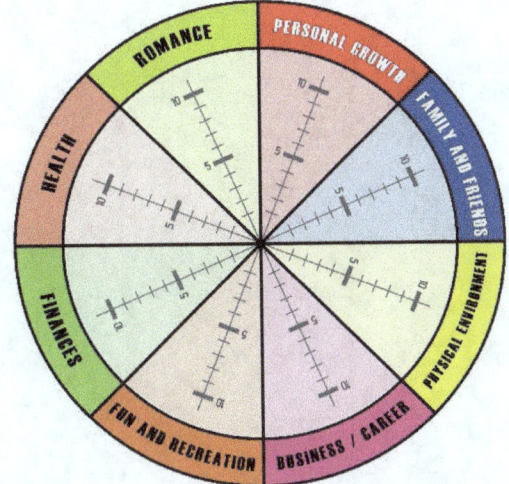

First, review the eight categories on your Wheel of Life. Don't get caught up on the labels in the categories. If necessary, they can be relabeled or split, or you can add something you think is missing.

Here are some examples of alternate labels:

Family and Friends: split into separate categories.

Significant Other: Dating, Relationship, or Life Partner.

Career: Motherhood, Work, Business, Volunteering

Finances: Money, Financial Security, Financial Well-Being

Health: Emotional, Physical, Fitness, Spiritual Well-Being

Home Environment: can be split or changed to the work environment for career or business.

Fun and Leisure: can be changed to Learning or Self-Development.

Others to Add: Security, Service, Leadership, Achievement, Community.

Now, rank your level of satisfaction with each area of your life by placing a value between 1 (very dissatisfied) and 10 (fully satisfied)

Career/Money

- Is my job rewarding?

- Do I earn enough and live within my means?

- Does it reflect my values?

- Do I save enough?

- Do I have the opportunity for advancement?

- Am I planning for financial freedom?

Health

- Do I eat healthily?

- Do I exercise regularly?

- Am I generally fit and well?

Significant Other/Romance

- Do I have/desire a life partner?

- Do we share values and intimacy?

- Am I nurturing the relationship we have with each other?

Friends and Family

- Do I have/desire a close circle of friends?

- Do I spend enough time with family and friends?

- Do I value the relationship we have with each other?

Personal Growth

- Am I continually learning new things?

- Do I enjoy new growth opportunities?

- Are the things I do growing me as a person?

Fun and Recreation

- Do I have fun often?

- Do I know how to relax?

- Do I enjoy or have hobbies?

Physical Environment

- Is my home comfortable?

- Do I like the area in which I live?

 ***EMPOWERful Questions***

How do you feel about your life as you look at your wheel?

_____

_____

_____

_____

What would a score of 10 look like/feel like?

_____

_____

_____

_____

Which of these categories would you most like to improve?

_____

_____

_____

_____

How could you make space for these changes in your life?

_____

_____

_____

_____

If there was one key action you could take to begin to bring everything in balance, what would it be?

_____

_____

_____

_____

_____

Time to take action! It's not just knowing the information but also having to do something with it. I want you to now identify one action step for each area, even if you are already at a 10 in the area. If picking an action step for each category is too much right now, don't worry, you can start with three areas you want to work on and identify an action step.

What is the smallest step you can take to get started? Taking small consistent steps is the key because small steps every day go a long way.

TOP 3 AREAS:

1. _____

2. _____

3. _____

ACTION STEPS

1. _____

2. _____

3. _____

Why Is the Question

Whether we achieve our goals depends on whether we take action. What is impacted if you take action? How bad do you want it? How motivated are you? If you are unclear about why it is important to you, how likely will you do what you must to achieve the goal or get your breakthrough?

Sometimes we do things for the wrong reasons. I know I've been guilty of that. I'm inviting you to try something new in a new way. Now we will do things that are in alignment. It may take a bit to dig deep and figure that out but that's what I'm here for. The next exercise is one I use with my clients to help them get clear on the *why* of their goal.

We all have goals we want to achieve, like losing weight, making more money, finding true love, improving the love we have, getting a promotion, gaining more confidence, etc. But have you ever thought about *why* you wanted these things? When you get these things and accomplish your goals, what does that mean for your life?

Later in the book, you'll be learning more about motivation and determining key motivational factors and tools, but it is important to get you to start thinking about what deeper motives are behind what you are doing and what you desire. If you're not motivated or inspired and haven't followed through in the past, it may be because you need *clarity* or to *dream bigger*! You want your goal(s) to not just be something you'd "like" to do. It's not a preference, it's not even a dream, it's a *must*!

This exercise will help you get clear and focused and more motivated to slay the goals you have for your beautiful life. Let's explore it now. Examine the goals you identified and ask yourself *why* you want this goal. What does it give you? When you get your answer, write it down and ask yourself this same question again, and then write it down once more so that you get to the core of what you *really* want. Ask yourself the same question once again then finally ask yourself, "What will this goal help me *feel?*" Access that. That's what we are searching for. What is the feeling you want to have? It's your choice. You have the power. You get to create it. You must make a creed with yourself; you must declare that it is your desire and embody it for yourself. In the next section, you get to do that.

_____

_____

_____

_____

_____

_____

_____

_____

_____

_____

_____

_____

_____

_____

_____

Creating a Vision and a Mission Statement

Having a mission statement is a concept I learned from a life coach. I found so much value in simply writing it out because it helps define who you are as a person and identifies your purpose, whether that's professionally or simply in life. It explains how you aim to pursue that purpose, and why it matters so much to you. After looking at the greater purpose behind your goals, take some time to see and feel yourself *living* your dreams. Put together a mission statement really captures and helps you visualize the end goal you have inspiring what you are doing.

Basic rules for writing a vision:

- Include various aspects of life.

- Write the tone and wording of your vision using **The Four P's**

  1. **P**ersonal (I, me statements)

  2. **P**resent (as if it's already happening, not future)

  3. **P**ositive (avoid words like "not" or "don't")

  4. **P**assion (put emotion into it)

Do a free writing activity where you spend at least five minutes writing all the details of the ideal life you see and desire. Write as many things as possible that come to you. In writing, focus more on the positive changes you have made than on the absence of some of the things that have annoyed you. Imagine the new situation you are in and describe the actions you have taken to improve your situation and to create a new quality of life and the benefits this has brought for you.

_____

_____

_____

_____

_____

_____

_____

_____

_____

_____

_____

_____

Now, make a summarized, one-paragraph version. In your paragraph, be sure to comment not just on your practical circumstances but your feelings, behaviors, and actions in this new world in which you are living. Also comment on how your needs and values are now being met and on any positive changes to the other areas of your life if these were not your primary area of focus but you have benefited. For example, you may have changed your career and found that feeling relaxed has had a positive effect on your relationships.

Sis, your vision of the future can be very ambitious, and it must be possible. If for example, you would like to recreate something you had in the past that is no longer possible or within your control, then it may be that instead, you will do best by trying to accept this and create a new future, without losing your memories of the past time or important situation which forms a part of your life and has contributed significantly to the unique human being that you are now.

Enjoy it and have some fun. Be bold, be creative, be _you_!

_____

_____

_____

_____

_____

_____

_____

_____

_____

_____

_____

Having this vision statement can be a great tool to reinforce those moments when you need extra motivation. You can also take your vision and make a physical representation of it, like with a physical or virtual photo vision board, which can further help you stay focused on the higher purpose behind what you are doing in your life.

Know Your Thrive Tribe

Accountability partners are people who have your back and can be counted on for encouragement and reinforcement of what you are trying to accomplish. These can be individuals who are friends, relatives, colleagues, business acquaintances, mentors, or coaches. These individuals do not necessarily have to be on the same path as you or share similar goals, but it does help to have at least one person who shares your interests and can better understand your challenges.

My life has been rich due to my _thrive tribe_. They have helped and supported me in numerous ways. My older sister is my rock and she's my person I can depend on. Also, two of my closest friends date back to junior and high school. That's over 35 years of friendship! We have grown up together. I've never had drama with my friends, never any messiness. I feel so blessed to have genuine and meaningful connections. They have seen and supported me at my lowest, clapped and celebrated me at my highest and everything in between. I also lean on the support of my therapist and life and business coaches.

Think of at least three people who would be a good source of accountability and commit to sharing your goals with at least one of them regularly.

1._____

2._____

3._____

Create a system where you can share your goals with your accountability partner, and they can share theirs. I would like to invite you to join our Members Only Facebook community, *Boss Ladies on a Journey to Limitless Possibilities*. It is another place for connecting. We meet weekly live and 365/24/7 in the group.

The key is to meet and talk regularly with your thrive tribe. The purpose is to share your intentions and goals, and then because you *know* that someone is going to be asking you about how things are going on a certain date, it keeps you motivated to have something to report back to them. You can share what you will be working on today, your weekly plan, or even your bigger vision. This doesn't mean you have to talk to them every day, but at least weekly is optimal to discuss what is going on and what you plan on doing for that week. This can be done in person, by phone, video chat, or through email. Doing this will help you stay heading in the right direction. Some of these individuals may even turn into collaborative partners.

A good example of an effective accountability partner is a workout buddy. If your goal is to get in shape or work out and you've decided to exercise regularly, having a workout partner join you when you exercise is a great idea. Then on the days you may not be feeling motivated (because they will come) and you feel like skipping the workout session, your partner will call you asking, "See you at 5?" You can also play this role for them.

Okay, maybe you don't have a physical partner; you can still have a tribe member who has similar fitness goals, and you can check in with each other at a predetermined time and this will also keep you going. For instance, knowing that on Wednesdays you'll be checking in with your accountability partner, you will not want to report that you skipped your boot camp class. This strategy works well for any goal.

Complete the accountability strategy exercises below.

Who and what are you accountable to?

1._____

2._____

3._____

What strategies will you use to hold yourself accountable?

1._____

2._____

3._____

Reflecting on the three people you identified as your accountability partners, what specific qualities or experiences do you believe make them worthy of this role in your journey? Furthermore, do you feel these individuals will challenge you constructively and will hold you accountable, or are they more likely to let you slide when it comes to your commitments and goals?

1._____

2._____

3._____

What system will you use with these people (time frame for meetings, place, and/or what will be shared)?

1._____

2._____

I Am Committed and Will Enjoy the Journey

Saying you are committed and *being* committed are two different things. Massive transformation requires a level of honesty with oneself and holding oneself accountable for your actions, and therefore your outcomes. In the journey of self-development, the best way to get results is to lean on your thrive tribe and when no one is around, the girl in the mirror has to keep it moving and still push through.

Accountability is a tool to help you keep commitments. You have already discovered your WHY in the previous section so now is the time to get clear with yourself that you are committed to this. *Why?* Well, it's your own *why.* What I can say is, whatever your *why i*s, you are important enough, worthy enough, kind enough, and smart enough to make yourself a priority and to make your life the best life you have because your *why* matters.

Commitment can be scary, I know. It can seem so final at times. Why do some people fear commitment? Because they misunderstand what commitment *is.* Commitment is *not* an obligation-something we do because we "should" or we "have to". Commitment *is* choice, dedication, and investment - something we are determined to do because we are motivated and inspired by genuine desire.

What would happen to your life if you put your *whole* self in? The value of commitment is that it keeps you moving forward even when the inevitable roadblocks and challenges cross your path. We're not talking about doing something out of obligation and then depending on willpower to follow through, we're talking about giving 110% dedication to that which you have a deep, genuine desire to do. What is it that you have a *powerful* enough reason to commit?

The first commitment you make to yourself is to *do* the activities in this book. Don't skip anything. Just reading this book will not change your life. It only works if you *take action and be intentional*!

What does "commitment" feel like to you?

_____

_____

_____

_____

What would happen to your life if you put your whole self in?

_____

_____

_____

_____

What is it that you have a powerful enough reason to commit to?

_____

_____

_____

_____

The cornerstone of success is the tools and systems in place. A product, a smart person, or a bright idea is only as good as its system. During the EMPOWER journey, you will need to track your work. Get yourself a journal, or better yet, an *I Choose Me Unapologetically* journal.

Remember! These tools are only as effective as you make them...and there are no limits if you're committed to following through. As a high achiever, I used to thrive with lists. I loved a good list I could scratch off and see my progress. Now with everything so electronic I don't always get the scratch-off satisfaction, but I certainly have the psychological satisfaction of seeing my goals and tasks accomplished. When we fulfill a goal, our brains release feel-good chemicals of satisfaction. It's kind of like giving yourself a Facebook 'like'. Our brain releases endorphins when we get social media 'likes'. So do yourself a favor and give yourself your own 'like' by doing something that not only will give you an instant boost of endorphins but will also get you closer to your goal.

I like to say to myself, "Ta Da!" *Ta Da* means 'Yep, I'm da bomb, job well done!' :) Or, if I'm feeling good, I may say, "Ta Dow! How you like me now?" Words from Ice Cube. Whatever your phrase is, just get into it.

Now, time for the commitment! Make a commitment to a weekly planning session at the beginning of the week or on Sunday night. Take a few minutes to determine what tasks you need to accomplish during the upcoming week to stay on track toward your goals. You will need a notebook, daily planner, calendar book, online smartphone, or even a whiteboard. Make a list of all the tasks you can think of that you intend to do in the coming week. If items need to be completed on a specific day, note this. If items are priorities that absolutely must be completed this week, star or highlight them and focus on these *first*.

As the week moves forward, it feels *great* to be able to cross items off the list. Keep them there, put a check, do not erase them. This helps you stay motivated by showing you what you've accomplished. Remember that sometimes life happens and not everything on your list for the week will get completed. That's okay, simply move it forward to next week!

A more effective way to manage your time is to devote, regularly, chunks of time to a specific project. Make it part of your schedule, your routine. This replaces to-do lists. The NY Times best-selling author and LEADx founder, Kevin Kruse, found that after interviewing over 200 billionaires, including Olympians, straight-A students, and entrepreneurs, they shared a similar trait. "Ultra-productive people don't work from a to-do list, but they do live and work from their calendar." Working from your calendar fights against perfectionism and procrastination, enhances concentration and focus, and ensures that you follow through with goals. If you increase your focus, getting more done in less time is the likely outcome.

Keep in mind how various strategies can render different results. All systems may not feel like a good fit for everyone, and what works for one person may feel clunky to another. Be flexible with yourself and be mindful that the more efficient your system is, the better results you'll get.

Where are you going to display and track your action list?

- Daily planner

- Whiteboard where it can be seen.

- In a planning or task app

Scheduling Your Weekly Strategy Session

Choose a time when you will sit down for 20-30 minutes every week to plan the coming week's tasks.

Weekly planning sessions will be held on: _____(day) at:_____(time)

Weekly Ta-Da /Tadow List

- IDENTIFY TASKS: Break down your sub-goals or tasks further. List *all* the tasks you'll need to do this week.

- PRIORITIZE: Identify which tasks are a priority (mark 1 through 5) and plan to do Level 1 *first*.

- PLAN: Schedule any tasks that are time-framed and assign another task to specific days of the week, when required. Keep the rest of your week's list somewhere easily accessible to refer to throughout the week when identifying daily goals.

Daily Plan

Keep going, things are gonna fall into place, I promise! You may not understand your obstacles right now but eventually, you will, and it will all make sense.

EMPOWER

CHAPTER 2

Educate - Understanding Yourself

This chapter is all about getting educated on why we do what we do when we are doing it. In this section, you will learn more about how beliefs are developed, and how our beliefs and coping skills can sabotage our growth, success, and happiness. Most importantly you'll understand the connection of thoughts, feelings, stress, and overall health and what you can do to take charge of your life.

Understand Your Thoughts and Become the Master of You

As a trained and experienced therapist, I have taught countless clients the science of their emotions in an easy-to-digest manner so they can:

1. Identify and have an awareness of them.

2. Be open and intentional about challenging them.

3. Try something new.

Many of us have something that has impacted us from our past. It could be hurt, abuse, and disappointments from our childhood. Perhaps you've experienced the loss of a loved one or a relationship. Most of my clients in my mental health practice have some history of childhood trauma. I see it not only in them but certainly in the past at myself. Unhealed childhood trauma can turn into anxiety and depression, as well as:

Low sense of self-worth	Poor decision making	Fear of abandonment
Resisting positive change	Codependency	Not prioritizing your own needs
Fixing others	External validation needed	Difficulty setting boundaries

People pleasing	Living on high alert	Tolerating abusive partner

These are some possible outcomes when you've endured childhood trauma. In fact, the more instances of trauma you experience, the likelihood of you having some of these concerns rises as proved in a study on the impact of childhood trauma. Your ACE's (Adverse Childhood Experience) score is a measure of the traumatic experiences you may have encountered during your childhood. These experiences can include physical, emotional, or sexual abuse, neglect, household dysfunction, witnessing domestic violence, and/or a parent with substance abuse, mental illness, or incarceration.

The impact of ACE's can be significant and far-reaching, affecting various aspects of your life and relationships. Here are some potential effects:

1. **Physical health**: High ACE scores have been linked to a range of physical health problems later in life such as heart disease, obesity, diabetes, and other chronic illnesses. Adverse childhood experiences can disrupt the body's stress response system, leading to long-term physiological changes that increase the risk of health issues.

2. **Mental and emotional well-being**: ACEs can have a profound impact on mental health. They are associated with a higher risk of developing mental health disorders like depression, anxiety, PTSD (post-traumatic stress disorder), substance abuse, and suicidal tendencies. Childhood trauma can affect emotional regulation and coping mechanisms.

3. **Relationships with others**: Adverse childhood experiences can influence your ability to form and maintain healthy relationships. Trauma can affect attachment patterns, trust, and intimacy, making it difficult to establish secure connections with others. People with high ACE scores may struggle with issues such as low self-esteem, fear of abandonment,

difficulty in expressing emotions, and challenges in establishing boundaries.

4. **Parenting and family dynamics**: ACEs can impact parenting skills and family dynamics. Those who have experienced trauma in childhood may find it more challenging to provide a nurturing and supportive environment for their own children. Unresolved trauma can lead to ineffective parenting strategies, emotional distance, and patterns of abuse or neglect, perpetuating the cycle of adverse experiences across generations.

5. **Educational and occupational outcomes**: ACEs can have a lasting impact on educational achievement and occupational success. The effects of trauma may manifest as difficulties with concentration, memory, and emotional regulation, affecting academic performance. Additionally, the emotional and psychological consequences of ACEs can influence job performance, career choices, and overall professional development.

While our childhood experiences can set the stage and our pasts can influence us, your past is not in control of the present (unless you let it). With proper support, therapy, and resilience-building strategies, individuals with high ACE scores can work towards healing and overcoming the negative impacts of their past experiences.

Awareness is key. Past experiences shape our "inner critic." Your inner critic thinks it's helping you, but it can be the thief that steals your joy, vision, passions, dreams, and meaningful connections. Your inner critic is the generator of ANTs- Automatic Negative Thoughts. Just like the insect, ANTs are small, will multiply, and can get out of control. ANTs call for backup, more and more come and before you know it, they are running all over the place. Time to get some Raid and exterminate those small annoyances for good!

Once you can understand and challenge the thought that's not serving you and replace it with thoughts that do serve and elevate you, you're on your way to achieving mastery of your emotions. ANTs are also known as cognitive distortions, a way of thinking where some aspects of ideas and experiences are given more weight and focus than others. When we are operating in the space of our inner critic, one of these cognitive distortions is likely running the play. We make things out far worse than they are, making problems larger than life, which feels difficult or "impossible" to overcome. Take a look at the column which illustrates the many ways we muck things up with our distorted thinking. The right side of the column gives examples of what you can try in place of the ANT.

Possible rigid types of thinking	What you can try to do
Catastrophizing This is when the importance of a problem is exaggerated, or the worst possible outcome is assumed to be true. *I'll never be able to pay off my student loans. I'll be in debt forever!*	-what if things aren't as bad as I make them out to be? -how likely is it that this worry will come true? -if your worry does come true, what's the worst that could happen?
Black and White thinking This involves for example thinking that a situation is either perfect or else it's hopeless, using extreme terms to describe everything: always and never, easy and impossible. *I always mess up when I speak in public, I'll never be able to give a good presentation.*	-think of some in-between possibilities, if you can. -being able to find more than one possibility or solution. -recognize that you may not have all the information needed to understand the situation fully.
Mind Reading This involves, for example assuming that others are thinking certain things about you or doing things for a particular reason. *He's definitely judging me right now. I can see it in his eyes.*	-try to generate some alternative possible explanations for what the other person is doing or saying. -imagine purely for the sake of argument that you are right about the explanation of the other person's behavior. Try to clarify for yourself why that matters so much to you.

Fortune Telling This involves predicting how things will happen, either in an overly gloomy way or in an overly optimistic way. *I'm definitely going to fail this exam. I can feel it.*	-check that your prediction is supported by evidence. -remind yourself of other possibilities. -acknowledge that sometimes the future is not completely predictable.
Overgeneralization where a person assumes an experience from one event will apply to other events or to make excessively vague or general statements about something or someone. This involves saying things like: *You always, I'm always…' 'You never, I'll never…'* *I'll always be alone. I'll never find someone who truly loves me.*	-focus on the issue, not the person. Instead of saying "you always," focus on the specific behavior or action that is causing the problem. -avoid sweeping statements. Instead of saying "no one," recognize that there may be individuals who do not fit into your generalization. -the same applies to self-critical statements.
Labeling people and situations Think of labeling like Generalization 2.0. Labeling is when you place a negative label on something, someone, or yourself entirely. It's extreme and hurtful. *She's a total flake. She's always late and never follows through on her commitments.*	-remember that people and even situations are complex. -allow for degrees and the possibilities (including you) may be good at some things and not so good at others. -allow the other person to be imperfect. -equally allow yourself to be imperfect.
Making demands This involves using words like "must", "should", and "ought" *I should always be friendly.* *I should always sacrifice for others.* *She ought to be grateful for what I've done.*	-try to avoid dogmatic words like 'must' and 'should' which impose a demand on others or yourself. Instead, reflect your feelings and wishes. -ask yourself, "Will it be helpful if I impose demands or expectations?" An alternative might be to make a request or slightly lower your expectations of the other person or yourself.
Magnification and Minimization Exaggerating the importance or positive attribute of another while minimizing your own. *He's really not that great. I could do so much better than him if I just had the chance.*	-what if I believed I was deserving and capable? -what if I believed the positive attribute to be true about myself?

Personalization	-who else could or what else could have played a part in this?
Personalization is when you entirely blame yourself, or someone else, for a situation that, in reality, involved many factors that were out of your control.	-you could try to see the argument from the other person's perspective and recognize that it's not all thier fault.
It's all my fault that the project failed. I should have done a better job.	-you can acknowledge that you made a mistake, but instead of dwelling on it, you can focus on what you learned from the experience and how you can improve in the future.
She's the one who caused the argument. She's always so difficult to deal with.	
Filtering	-instead of focusing on the one negative aspect of the situation, you could try to see the bigger picture and recognize the positive aspects too.
Takes the negative and magnifies it and disqualifies the positive.	-you could try to gather more information and consider multiple perspectives before jumping to conclusions.
I got all these great comments on my evaluation, but the one negative comment is all I can think about.	- you could remind yourself that one negative experience or comment doesn't define your entire life or identity.
Emotional Reasoning	-Instead of assuming that your emotions reflect the way things really are, you could try to separate your feelings from the facts.
The assumption that emotions reflect the way things really are.	-you could recognize that your emotions are temporary and may not reflect the whole picture.
I feel like a bad friend, therefore I am a bad friend.	-you could remind yourself that your emotions are not the only truth, and that there may be other perspectives and factors to consider.

Having negative thoughts is normal, believing them when there is no basis for them is dangerous. Our mind is a weapon, and we use it against ourselves more often than not. This way of thinking is total nonsense. Until I recognized what I was doing, the distortions that dictated my life were mind reading and personalization. I walked around with a chip on my shoulder. I assumed people were judging me, talking about me negatively and I needed to protect myself from people's BS. I was friendly but I had armor on to protect me. To avoid criticism, I strived to get things right. After all, getting things right, like getting good grades, resulted in being praised and rewarded for my efforts and I liked that feeling the most. When I was younger, my report cards would be the source of the positive attention and affirmation I received. I especially remember how I felt when my biological mother, Cookie, would appear proud of my accomplishments. I do believe she was proud; however, she also benefited from my scholarly strengths. Cookie would take my report cards and go around and collect money from her friends and different men for my straight "E's." In elementary, the grading scale they used was E for excellent, G for good, S for satisfactory, N for needs improvement, and U for unacceptable. It didn't matter to me that she collected the money, it was the feeling of acceptance that I craved. This need to be accepted and seen would follow me throughout my adolescence and well into and through my adulthood.

Our early development sets the stage for things like perfectionism. Brene Brown has this to say about perfectionism: "It is the 20-pound shield we lug around hoping it protects us from experiencing judgment, shame, and blame when all it really does is keep us from being seen…And it's heavy AF." The abandonment I felt from both my mother and father, but especially from my mother, developed into my hyper-independence. Hyper-independence is the result of trauma. Statements like, "I don't need anyone" and "I'll just do it myself" (my old favorite line) really mean that my ability to trust has been injured by people systemically failing me and letting me down. But we do need people. Thinking we don't is the result of cognitive distortion.

Take a look at another list of disparaging statements. Which one have you said or presently say to yourself?

"I feel like I'm up against the world."	"I can't get things together."
"No one understands me."	"My life is a hot mess."
"I've let people down."	"I'll never make it."
"I'm so disappointed in myself."	"I can't finish anything."
"I can't get started."	"Why can't I ever find somebody?"
"What's wrong with me?"	"I'm not as smart/creative/attractive as others."

Do any of these sound familiar? What ANT or ANTs are running amuck in your life?

In challenging this thing, take action. Think of a scenario where you responded with an ANT. Maybe you have examples of all the distortions or maybe it's just one. No matter how many or little distortions you have, they *will* have adverse results in your life. In your journal, give one example, whether current or in the past, from each type of rigid and distorted thinking pattern. For each example, you should describe a particular situation where you found yourself thinking in the rigid/distorted way listed in the left-hand column. Describe the situation, what you thought, and the outcome. Once you complete that, read through the responses and decide whether you want to try out any of the options listed for dealing with each type of rigid distorted thinking.

DESCRIBE THE SITUATION	YOUR THOUGHTS	OUTCOME

We grow when we ask ourselves reflective questions *and* answer them truthfully. Listed below are some EMPOWERful questions. I call them EMPOWERful because it takes you to rely on *you* to give yourself the authority to have the confidence to do something in *your* life.

Let's say you invited a good friend to your girls' brunch. She never showed up and she wasn't answering her phone or texts. You felt irritated, concerned, and worried. Is she avoiding you? Did she forget? Did she get into an accident?

What evidence is there to show that my understanding of this situation is accurate? (Using our example, my friend didn't show up and didn't text or call.)

_____

_____

_____

_____

_____

Is there another way of looking at this? There may be evidence to support an alternative explanation.

_____

_____

_____

_____

_____

_____

_____

3. What would be so bad if my initial understanding proved to be accurate?

_____

_____

_____

_____

_____

4. *How do I cope if this really is the case?*

_____

_____

_____

_____

_____

_____

5. *What are the consequences of believing my understanding to be accurate? Positive and/or negative consequences?*

_____

_____

_____

_____

_____

_____

_____

6. *How can I change or accept my understanding, after weighing all the evidence, to make it less distressing?*

_____

_____

_____

_____

_____

_____

_____

7. *What does this mean for me? What is the impact?*

_____

_____

_____

_____

_____

_____

Now It's Time to Take Massive Action

Time to shift from the 'stinkin' to 'thinkin'. Dump the garbage mindset and embrace a growth mindset. This can be done. It's going to take effort and lots of practice, every day. Our mindset, aka our 'belief system', is fluid and can be shifted and you have the capacity to do it!

Next, we are going to take some rigid/distorted types of thinking and flip them. Another way of overcoming these thoughts is to approach them with this easy-to-remember method.

Each step starts with an 'E' for *Empower*.

1. **Examine.** Seek evidence for or against the thought.

Does an occurrence make it a fact?

2. **Explore** the meaning.

Could there be another explanation?

3. **Expose** for authenticity.

Is it distorted or biased?

4. **Expand** your perspective.

Shift your mindset.

5. **Experiment.** What's a different thought and behavior?

Try it out.

6. **Empowered** by your courage.

Celebrate yourself for moving out of your comfort zone.

Stress and Its Impact

Stress is normal for everyone. I can guess that stress is a concept you're very familiar with. You're a high achiever, you have a demanding job/career or a demanding academic load, coupled with juggling ten other things, (side hustle, bae, kids, parents, social life, organizations, etc), so I get it.

You have a choice about stressful situations. We are in control of how we respond to situations, and the way we respond is paramount to our overall health. I know I'm not the first to tell you that stress has massive implications for your physical and mental health.

As a Black woman, my stress has manifested into emotional concerns. I have had both depression and anxiety. Sure, it was hard for others to see; I was high-functioning. Just like there are high-functioning alcoholics, there are those who can mask their depression, anxiety, and other mental health struggles.

I am not alone in this; depression and anxiety can manifest differently in individuals, regardless of race or gender. However, when considering the experiences of Black women, it's important to recognize that we face unique challenges and stressors that can contribute to our mental health struggles. Here are some common aspects to consider:

1. Sociocultural Factors: Black women often face systemic racism, discrimination, and inequality, which can lead to chronic stress, feelings of marginalization, and a sense of not belonging. These factors can contribute to the development or exacerbation of depression and anxiety.

2. Intersectionality: Black women often experience the intersection of multiple forms of discrimination, including racism and sexism. This intersectionality can compound the stressors they face and impact their mental health.

3. Stigma and Cultural Barriers: In some cultural communities, mental health issues may be stigmatized, and seeking help may be perceived as a sign of weakness. This stigma can prevent Black women from seeking the support they need, leading to delayed or inadequate treatment.

4. Historical Trauma: The legacy of historical trauma, such as slavery, colonization, and racial violence, can have intergenerational effects on mental health. The cumulative impact of these experiences can contribute to depression and anxiety among Black women.

5. Health Disparities: Black women may face disparities in access to quality healthcare, including mental health services. This can result in delayed diagnosis, inadequate treatment, and reduced mental health support.

Oftentimes our failing health or our health crisis gets our attention. If you are not able to recognize your stress levels and eliminate them from your life, stress will become a slow death sentence. Stress wreaks havoc on your body and can be a vicious cycle and lead to a downward spiral fast. No matter if you've had some health problems in the past or you're fairly healthy, you *can* prevent *future* problems by eliminating stress from your life.

Many years ago, I had these major headaches every day. They weren't migraines yet they were really intense. This went on for months. I went to the doctor pleading for help. As drastic as this sounds, I thought I had a misdiagnosed tumor or something. Every day on my way home from work, like clockwork I would get this splitting headache. Just several minutes from arriving home and BANG, there it was. I would rest my head in my hands, rubbing my temples with Tiger Balm, trying to massage the pain away.

I'd pop my Advil daily like they were Tic Tac mints. I kept the extra-large bottle of Advil from Costco on deck. Unbeknownst to me, what was going on was my response to my home life. Shit was stressful at home. There was disappointment waiting for me, resentful feelings were waiting for me, and frustration and irritation were waiting for me. Lastly, it was my sense of hopelessness waiting for me as I just didn't know how I was going to get out of feeling like this. Stress is deadly and it will kill you. I was dying a slow mental death.

The effects of stress on your body are major. As I've gotten older and more knowledgeable of the effects of stress on the body, mind, and spirit, I don't play with it. I respect it. I had a client who, when she first started with me, complained about the amount of stress that was in her life. Her work life was very demanding, she was also finishing up her doctorate and continued to experience micro-aggression from her advisor at school, and one of her children was having challenges in school. Her stress resulted in her having a severe case of insomnia, which continued the cycle of her agitated, frustrated feelings, resulting in further fatigue and exhaustion. Stress affects people differently; this is not an exhaustive list of what's at risk but what's commonly seen as a result of stress. Take a look:

High Blood Pressure	Insomnia	Depression	High Blood Sugar
Stomachaches	Weakened Immune System	Risk of Heart Attack	Headaches
Heartburn	Missed Periods	Rapid Breathing	Tense Muscles

The bottom line is that the nervous system responds to stress by releasing a flood of adrenaline and cortisol into the body. Another term you may be familiar with is 'fight or flight'. This is when the body thinks there's a 'bear' and gets you ready to fight the bear or run from the bear, and for both of these actions, you need adrenaline and cortisol. However, there's no bear and yet, our bodies are paying the price for that fake bear. Just to break it down a bit more, here is what's going on with the physical body.

PHYSICAL

Muscle tension/headaches	Flushing (face feeling hot)
Sleep disturbance/tiredness	Prolonged/frequent headaches
Increased 'breakouts'	Susceptibility to mild illness
Rapid pulse	Dizziness/faintness
Nausea	Breathlessness/chest pain
Indigestion	Ongoing nausea/stomachache
Increased sweating	Ongoing fitful sleep

BEHAVIORAL

Appetite changes/compulsive eating	Change in sleeping patterns
Impatience, carelessness, hyperactivity	Increased alcohol, cigarette, and drug use
Poor productivity/low energy	Increased absenteeism, aggression, irritability
Avoidance of situations/places	Sudden tears

EMOTIONAL

Anxiety/sadness	Feelings of guilt and shame
Moodiness/grumpiness	Extreme anger (over-reaction)
Loss of sense of humor	Loss of libido
Withdrawal/feeling of isolation	Overwhelming feelings of panic/anxiety

Low self-esteem	Feeling helpless/hopeless

THOUGHTS/PERCEPTION

Inability to make decisions or muddled thinking	Over-sensitive to criticism
Reduced coordination/creativity	Poor concentration
Becoming more vague/forgetful	Negative self-talk/fear of failure
Negative 'globalization'. Everything seems to go wrong/is bad	Feelings of 'unfairness'
Fear of rejection/defensiveness	Can't switch off
Rushed decisions	Over-sensitive to criticism

I believe it's important to highlight that trauma can have a lasting impact on us as it lives in the body. If you are ever curious as to how this really happens, read *The Body Keeps the Score* by Bessel van der Kolk. When people say, "*It lives in the body*", one may question what this looks like. I've seen energy workers show different movements releasing "trauma from the hips" so some may have a misconception about how it's actually in the body. Trauma is not physically held in the muscles or bones; instead, the need to protect oneself from perceived threats is stored in the memory and emotional centers of the brain. This activates the body whenever a situation reminds the person of the traumatic event(s). Traumatic events push the nervous system outside its ability to regulate itself. For some, the system gets stuck in the "on" position, and the person is overstimulated and unable to calm down. Anxiety, anger, restlessness, panic, and hyperactivity can all result when you stay in this ready-to-react mode.

Releasing this pent-up energy and having an awareness of what your body is feeling is important. Crying can be seen as a negative action, but in fact, there are benefits to crying. It provides a releasing, self-soothing effect, it activates rest and digestion (parasympathetic nervous system), and it helps you receive the support you need from the people around you -milling et al 2016. It releases oxytocin and endorphins. Our endorphins are the happy chemicals we produce that ease emotional and physical pain. Crying also aids sleep, improves vision, and helps fight bacteria in our eyes.

How do you experience stress in your body?

_____

_____

_____

_____

What is The Bear in your life?

_____

_____

_____

_____

_____

Did you make the connections before? Did you consider the reason you were having some of these symptoms was because of unchecked stress, AKA The Bear?

_____

_____

_____

_____

_____

Which one is most important for you to control and overcome and why?

_____

_____

_____

_____

_____

_____

If you don't control and overcome your stress, what is the cost?

_____

_____

_____

_____

When we want to change a behavior, the body goes into the self-sabotage mode. The body does not want to move out of its comfort zone. Self-sabotage is **when people do (or don't do) things that block their success or prevent them from accomplishing their goals**. It can happen consciously or unconsciously. Self-sabotaging behaviors can affect our personal and professional success, as well as our mental health. Write about a time you sabotaged your efforts.

Did you achieve what you wanted?

_____

_____

_____

_____

_____

What could you have done to be successful?

_____

_____

_____

_____

_____

_____

_____

Love It /Loathe It

Doing things we enjoy is a no-brainer and we often are resistant to doing things we hate. The main reason to do what you love is your happiness. Finding that place not only provides contentment but also makes you more motivated. Now the opposite of that tale is the things you loathe. Have you ever analyzed the things you avoid the most? Do you know what they are?

In life, we do many things daily. Some of those things we do like we are robots on automation, some of what we are doing we generally enjoy doing, and some things we just wish we didn't have to do at all. When we can take a moment and an inventory of what it is we are doing in our lives, we are better equipped to shift our mindset and actions. Do more of what you love and less of what you hate. A shift in the way you look at a situation from "I have to do" to "I get to do" can improve your experience as well.

Focusing on things that bring you *joy* is the priority. When we do that, it can boost our immune systems, fight stress and chronic pain, and improve our chances of living a longer life. You will see that this topic of joy and creating joy in one's life is to me the most important thing we are tasked with in our beautiful lives. Throughout this workbook, you will see why creating joy in *all* aspects of your life is the *only* thing to focus on. Everything else follows. Throughout the week, as you go about your work and life, notice how you feel about your tasks and activities. If you love doing something, or it makes you feel good and energized, make a note of it under the "Love It" column. If you really dislike doing something or it makes you feel empty, aggravated, or bored, note that under the "Loathe It" column. At the end of the week, look at your list. Choose the top three that really resonated with you from the "Love It" list. These statements likely describe you at your very best. For example, "I love volunteering at my daughter's school", "I love gardening in my backyard", "I loved helping my company with an innovative project", or "I love going to my Zumba class." Move these statements from "love" language into a "strengths" language. Knowing that you can't volunteer at your daughter's school all the time/full time, you might write something like, "I feel good when I support youth academic success." or "I feel at peace and a great sense of accomplishment when I see my fruits and vegetables grow" or "I feel empowered when I contribute to advancing my team at work." or "I feel energized and healthy when I make time for my physical health and wellness." How might you play to your strengths more each week? Develop a list of "weakness" areas in a similar way. Begin to think about how you might work around or through those weaknesses or things you loathe – remembering that we are made to work with others as a team. Can you delegate some of the activities? Could you minimize the amount of time you spend in your areas of weakness? Would anyone notice or care if you walked away from it altogether? Perhaps someone strong in these areas could show you how to do these things more efficiently or effectively. Or that person might be willing to take on some of these tasks if you are willing to help in areas where they are weak, but you are strong.

One of the benefits of the pandemic was that I got to use delivery services such as Instacart. Instead of exposing myself to the virus and spending my precious time going to the grocery store, looking for a parking spot, shopping, standing in line, lugging my things to my car, unpacking, and putting them away once I got home, I omitted five of my six steps with just the push of a button. Winning! Sure, I enjoy picking out my own fruits and veggies and I still do it periodically; however, I enjoy the hours it frees up for me to do more of what I love.

In fact, delegating is one of the most important skills of a leader. We are not doing things as solo artists. As the African proverb says, "*You go by yourself, you go fast, you go with others, you go far."* I do a challenge called *Delegate Like a Boss* quarterly. The participants are mostly high-achieving women, executives, directors, CEOs, and entrepreneurs who may have a family and other interests. At the end of the challenge, they are skilled in eliminating burnout because they shift their mindset on what it means to be powerful. Work smart, not hard.

Time to make your Love/Loathe list. I encourage you to focus on your *Love* list. What makes you sing and smile? It's okay if you really can't sing, but that feeling when you want to sing! Imagine driving down the street or freeway and your favorite tune is on and you're just singing away like no one is watching or listening. Tap into those "feel good feelings".

LOVE IT	LOATHE IT
❖	❖
❖	❖
❖	❖
❖	❖
❖	❖

What Is the Negative, Limiting Belief or "Story" That You Are Telling Yourself?

Changing our beliefs is not only possible but also necessary. Making changes is a natural life occurrence. Oftentimes limiting beliefs are passed down to us by the attitudes and beliefs of others. I was raised partially by "Mama" who was from the old school. Being that she was from a much older generation, lots of her ways and beliefs about the world I adopted. Some were beneficial and some, not so much. In addition, I got some of my beliefs from my biological mother, Cookie. One belief that I got from my mama is that education is important as a Black person and once you get your education, it is something no one can ever take away from you. I really ingrained that one in my belief system and it is one that I have kept. However, there have been others that are limiting and not necessarily relevant to my situation. Below I'm going to share with you some common phrases that we were often told when we were growing up. They are so frequently used we rarely question their validity or consider how they are impacting our belief systems. Remember, as children, we are sponges, absorbing and sucking up everything around us. We are being informed on how to act and respond based on our environment. I wholeheartedly believe there were good intentions behind several of them, but I challenge you to reconsider these mindset roadblocks.

In my journey, I now know my power and how powerful my thoughts are. I made an agreement with myself that I am worthy of everything I want, including extreme joy. I made peace with myself to stop finding fault with myself. I stopped looking for reasons to feel bad and I started looking for reasons to feel good. I eliminated catastrophizing everything in my life and looked towards optimism. But most importantly, I stopped asking permission from others and looking to others to be the reason why I felt good, and I decided that I could be the reason for my feeling good and in that decision, I found the ultimate freedom. *I* get to choose. Damn…that feels good. Nobody can dictate that for me.

Pay close attention to the potential risks when having these beliefs.

- *Money is the root of all evil.*: Unconsciously avoiding or sabotaging financial success to avoid the "negative qualities" you believe you'll develop if you have money.

- *Money doesn't grow on trees.* Not believing you can have what you want if it involves having money and therefore not going for it.

- *Don't burn your bridges.* This means not making a change or taking an opportunity when it comes out of fear of disappointing, offending, or otherwise burning a bridge.

- *No pain, no gain.* Choosing not to make changes or go for what you want because you feel it will be difficult or painful, holding yourself back from success. This can also lead to sabotaging to make a situation harder than it has to be.

- *Life is hard.* Feeling discouraged and hopeless: accepting difficulties or unnecessary suffering because you believe it is normal or expected.

- *Good things come to those who wait.* A feeling of impatience due to focusing on the length of time and not doing something you want because it will "take too long". It can also lead to not taking the steps that would create rapid results because it would make us question the statement if it worked.

- *You have to pay your dues.* Feeling unworthy, you may not take opportunities, or you may punish yourself for rewards and accomplishments you receive with ease.

- *I gotta do it all by myself because I can't depend on anyone, and they won't get it right anyway.* This can be an indication of hyper-independence, which is a result of trauma. Statements and feelings like this really mean *my ability to trust has been injured by people systematically failing me and letting me down*. At the end of the day, we need people.

- *I'm not doing enough.* This belief revolves around feeling inadequate or unworthy, leading to self-doubt and a lack of confidence.

- *I'm ugly/ I'm fat.* These negative statements relate to poor body image and self-esteem. You might feel dissatisfied with your physical appearance, comparing yourself unfavorably to societal beauty standards or others around you.

- *I don't deserve success.* Believing that success, happiness, or abundance are meant for others but not for yourself can create a self-imposed barrier to achieving goals.

- *I'm too old/young.* Age-related beliefs can hinder personal and professional growth, making you feel like you are either too inexperienced or past your prime to pursue your aspirations.

- *I'm not smart/talented enough.* The belief that intelligence or talent is fixed and cannot be developed can limit you from challenging yourself or acquiring new skills.

- *It's too risky.* Fear of failure or uncertainty can prevent you from taking risks, trying new things, or pursuing opportunities that may lead to personal or professional growth.

- *I must please everyone.* The belief that one must always meet expectations and gain approval from others can result in people-pleasing behavior, sacrificing personal needs and boundaries.

- *I can't change.* Believing that personal change or growth is impossible can lead to complacency and hinder personal development.

- *I must be perfect.* Striving for perfection can lead to excessive self-criticism, fear of failure, and a reluctance to take action due to the fear of making mistakes.

- *I'm a victim.* Believing that external circumstances or other people control one's life can lead to a sense of powerlessness and prevent you from taking responsibility for your own actions and choices.

- *I'm a burden.* Believing that you are too much to handle or that you impose on others. This negative statement often arises from low self-worth and can contribute to feelings of isolation and withdrawal.

Which of these phrases were you conditioned to believe? Can you think of others? Can you see any fear you developed because of them? Can you see any way in which they have limited you? Where did the idea(s) come from? Are you sure it's true? Who told you this? Are you sure they were right? Do you have evidence that goes against these limiting beliefs? If you can't prove these limiting beliefs true beyond a reasonable doubt, can you discard them?

When you get over your limiting beliefs, a world of possibilities opens up to you. Here are some of the things that become possible:

- *Personal Growth.* Overcoming limiting beliefs allows you to tap into your full potential and pursue personal growth. You become more open to learning, trying new things, and taking on challenges. This leads to continuous improvement and self-development.

- *Increased Confidence*. Letting go of limiting beliefs boosts your confidence and self-esteem. You start believing in your abilities and talents, which enables you to take risks and pursue your goals with greater enthusiasm. As a result, you become more resilient in the face of adversity.

- *Expanded Opportunities*. Limiting beliefs often hold us back from seizing new opportunities. Overcoming those beliefs makes you more open-minded and receptive to possibilities. You may be more likely to explore new career paths, start a business, or pursue ventures you previously deemed impossible.

- *Stronger Relationships.* Limiting beliefs can affect how we perceive others and our ability to connect with them. By overcoming these beliefs, you become more understanding, empathetic, and accepting. This can lead to stronger and more fulfilling relationships with friends, family, and colleagues.

- *Creativity and Innovation*. Limiting beliefs can stifle your creativity and prevent you from thinking outside the box. When you let go of these beliefs, you become more open to new ideas and perspectives. This allows you to tap into your creative potential and come up with innovative solutions to problems.

- *Improved Health and Well-Being*. Limiting beliefs can create stress, anxiety, and negative emotions. Overcoming them can lead to improved mental and emotional well-being. You may experience reduced stress levels, increased happiness, and a more positive outlook on life. This, in turn, can have a positive impact on your physical health.

- *Success and Achievement*. Limiting beliefs often hold us back from pursuing our dreams and goals. By overcoming them, you empower yourself to strive for success and achievement. You become more willing to take on challenges, persist in the face of obstacles, and reach for higher levels of accomplishment.

It's important to note that overcoming limiting beliefs is a process that requires self-reflection, self-awareness, and consistent effort. But by working on them, you can unlock your full potential and create a life filled with possibilities.

I have had several times in my life I doubted myself. Every single day I have to be intentional in keeping the doubts at bay. Even during the writing of the book, I felt like a rock was ready to fall off the cliff and smash me like the cartoon, Wile E. Coyote. Doubt is such a strange thing. There will be times when you succeed and there will be times when you will fail so wasting your time doubting whether you're gonna be successful or not is pointless. It is just putting one foot in front of the other. You control what you can control, and then you see what the outcome is. If you win, great! You're gonna have to wake up the next day and do the journey all over again. And if you lose, oh well, you're gonna have to wake up the next day and do the journey all over again anyway.

Keep in mind when I say "lose" or "fail" I am not looking at it negatively and most of us do. We internalize it and feel like something is wrong with us. In fact, a "fail or lose" is in my book a *win* because it's a lesson, and lessons provide knowledge and give us an opportunity to grow. But that's a mindset shift. That's a new belief I have but it wasn't always like that. I encourage you to challenge yourself and challenge your beliefs. Examine if they are still relevant in your life. Is it holding you back or propelling you forward? How are you viewing your "failures"? "Failures" can actually have several benefits. Here are some of them:

1. *Learning and Growth.* Failures provide valuable learning experiences. When we fail, we gain insights into what went wrong, what didn't work, and what we could have done differently. This knowledge helps us grow personally and professionally and enables us to make better decisions in the future.

2. *Resilience and Perseverance.* Failure often tests our resilience and ability to bounce back. It teaches us to persevere in the face of challenges and setbacks. By experiencing failure and overcoming it, we develop the strength to handle adversity and become more resilient individuals.

3. *Innovation and Creativity.* Failures can be catalysts for innovation and creativity. When our efforts don't yield the desired results, we are encouraged to think outside the box, explore new approaches, and come up with innovative solutions. Failures can spark creativity and lead to breakthroughs that may not have been possible otherwise.

4. *Humility and Self-Reflection.* Failure humbles us and reminds us that we are not infallible. It prompts self-reflection and introspection, allowing us to reassess our goals, values, and strategies. It helps us recognize our weaknesses and areas for improvement, fostering personal and professional growth.

5. *Reshaping Perspective.* Failure can shift our perspective and challenge our assumptions. It can help us question conventional wisdom and see things from different angles. By embracing failure, we become open to new possibilities and are more willing to take calculated risks.

It's important to note that while failures can be beneficial, they should not be sought out or glorified for their own sake. The key lies in learning from failures, adapting, and using the gained knowledge to improve future endeavors.

In conclusion, childhood trauma can impact many domains of one's life and will require intentional awareness of cognitive distortions, aka ANTs. Even if you don't have childhood trauma, ANTs are possible, and self-awareness is an ongoing practice. ANTs exacerbate internalized stress and living with chronic stress can have detrimental effects on our lives and well-being. Understanding and addressing ANTs, along with implementing effective stress management strategies, is essential for maintaining a healthy and balanced life. By doing so, you can cultivate resilience, improve your mental health, and enhance your overall quality of life. Know that you are not a prisoner of your past. You hold the key to experiencing the life you want. However, we can't transform and make shifts without awareness.

This is the first step in understanding "why" I act this way when the more compassionate question would be, 'What happened to me?' I encourage you to get curious and unpack it. Make room for what you want in there.

"Do the best you can until you know better. Then when you know better, do better."

Maya Angelou

EMPOWER

CHAPTER 3

Mindfulness - Calming Yourself

Understanding The Benefits and Core Skills of Mindfulness

In this chapter, you will learn different mindfulness techniques so you can live your life with an extra dose of energy to take on your toughest day, enjoy more leisure, and everything in between. With these techniques, you are encouraged to explore them and decide which ones feel most comfortable for you, and which ones seem right for you at this time in your life. Practice them and use them as a way of grounding yourself in the present. You are encouraged to develop your own mindfulness strategies. Use these strategies as a starting point. There is no right or wrong when it comes to mindfulness. There is no pass or fail. It works differently for everyone.

What is mindfulness and how will it change your life? I like to look at mindfulness in a few ways. One way of understanding mindfulness is that it is a distinct way of paying attention to the present moment. This could entail the present moment of experiencing yourself in your own body; your bodily, physical sensations that occur moment by moment. It may be an awareness in the present moment of your thoughts and emotions. It may be a present-moment awareness of the world around you, of the sights, sounds, smells, tastes, and tactile experience. It might be a moment-by-moment unfolding of awareness of a number of these elements simultaneously.

One of the things that characterize the practice of mindfulness is that it's not just noticing, it's also noticing and being aware in a particular way. It's observing with curiosity, without judgment, and without deciding whether a particular present-moment experience is right or wrong, good, or bad. Yes, there may be feelings of comfort or discomfort, but that doesn't mean the experience is 'bad' or 'good,' in and of itself.

Most of the time we live our lives 'mindlessly.' We are literally 'out of ourselves,' we are out of the present moment. We are thinking about the future, or we are worried about what has been going on recently in our lives, or we're having painful, difficult thoughts about the past. By cultivating and practicing mindfulness, we develop the capacity, which is in all of us, to come back to the present moment. When you think about it, ultimately the only time we can live in is in the present.

It took me to start working on my clinical license to learn about mindfulness. I know for me my goal in life, right now, at this moment, is to be genuinely happy and I have a mindset that whatever happens, happens. I don't fret about things and worry about the future or dwell in the past. If we think about the past, we're always thinking about the past from the present moment. If we're worrying about the future (and a good definition of anxiety is worrying about things that haven't yet happened), we actually still do that from the present moment. There has been a lot of research in recent years indicating the effectiveness of mindfulness practice. Mindfulness has been considered helpful for improving issues like depression, high levels of stress or distress, and anxiety. Mindfulness can be helpful for people who have experienced deeply painful traumatic events. Having said that, mindfulness is not a way of getting rid of the events, memories, or feelings associated with painful parts of life, but to move towards a place where there is less suffering because of these events. Perhaps you didn't even have a painful memory or suffering from the past. Mindfulness is about living and experiencing the here and now.

When I started to really pay attention and worked on my healing, I had to get quiet. I had to isolate myself. When you spend time alone you learn what makes you happy and you also learn all the things that you were doing to make other people happy while you were miserable. That's the deeper work. To start, think of mindfulness as an opportunity to slow down. For some people, it's about finding a quiet safe space and giving themselves 20 minutes, half an hour, or even longer, to become mindful. For others it might just be a few seconds or a minute at a time - many moments of checking in briefly with your experience in the 'here' and 'now.' Some days it may come more easily than others. Try not to judge yourself, or your performance, as you do these exercises. Just the experience of trying them out is an act of mindfulness, and that is sufficient.

If you try one of the exercises and it's not useful to you right then, don't let it concern you. Let it go. Coming back and trying later is indeed an option. If there's a particular one you do find useful, use it over and over. If you want to develop your own, using these exercises as a starting point, that's awesome. If at any point during these exercises, because of anything that is happening in your life at that moment, it becomes difficult to continue, simply stop. Look around you, acquaint yourself with your surroundings, and if you wish to come back to exercise later, or not, that's fine too. It's important, as you do these exercises, to be as gentle to yourself as possible. Use them for your own purposes. They're designed for *you*. Allow them to work for you.

Before we get to the exercises, here are the highlighted benefits of mindfulness:

1. **Stress reduction**. Mindfulness allows you to focus on the present moment, helping you let go of worries about the past or future. By cultivating a non-judgmental awareness of your thoughts and emotions, you can reduce stress and enhance your overall well-being.

2. **Improved mental health**. Mindfulness can be effective in managing and reducing symptoms of anxiety and depression. By observing your thoughts and emotions without judgment, you develop a greater capacity to respond to them skillfully and compassionately.

3. **Enhanced self-awareness**: Through mindfulness, you become more attuned to your

thoughts, emotions, and physical sensations. This self-awareness provides insights into your patterns of thinking and behavior, allowing you to make positive changes and cultivate a deeper understanding of yourself.

4. Increased focus and concentration. Regular mindfulness practice can enhance your ability to concentrate and sustain attention. By training your mind to stay present, you can improve your focus in various areas of life, such as work, study, or daily tasks.

5. Reduced rumination. Rumination is a common feature of many mental health disorders, particularly depression and anxiety. It involves repetitive and obsessive thinking about negative experiences or emotions. Mindfulness helps break the cycle of rumination by teaching individuals to observe their thoughts non-judgmentally and let them go. By reducing rumination, mindfulness can alleviate symptoms of depression and anxiety.

6. Improved emotional regulation. Mindfulness helps you develop a greater capacity to recognize and regulate your emotions. By cultivating a non-reactive and accepting stance towards your feelings, you can respond to them in a more balanced and constructive way, rather than being overwhelmed or controlled by them.

7. Better decision-making. Mindfulness cultivates a sense of clarity and perspective, enabling you to make more informed and considered decisions. By being fully present and aware, you can tap into your intuition and make choices that align with your values and goals.

8. Enhanced relationships. Mindfulness can improve your interactions with others. By being fully present and attentive during conversations, you can cultivate deeper connections, empathy, and understanding. Mindfulness also helps reduce automatic and judgmental reactions, leading to more compassionate and effective communication.

9. Increased overall well-being. Regular mindfulness practice can contribute to an increased sense of overall well-being and life satisfaction. By cultivating an attitude of acceptance, gratitude, and compassion, you can develop a more positive outlook on life.

Mindfulness is a skill that requires practice and patience. Integrating mindfulness into your daily life, whether through formal meditation or incorporating mindful moments throughout the day, can lead to significant benefits in various aspects of your life.

Learn and Practice Five Mindfulness Techniques

There are several mindfulness techniques and many of them are specifically aimed at addressing a concern. It is my opinion that mindfulness is necessary for women. Why? Women hold stress- we are the "superwomen" for friends and family, and mindfulness is the Kryptonite to stress. I'll be talking later about "Superwoman" as she's on the hit list and we'll be having a memorial for her. That woman is tired, exhausted, and worn out. As a Black woman, I'm certainly done with the strong Black woman narrative. Done!

The mindfulness techniques I'm sharing are aimed at aligning you with your present being and calming yourself when becoming dysregulated, whether that's during a charged conversation, microaggression, disrespectful neighbor, etc.

The 54321 Exercise

I love taking walks and if it's by some type of water, that's even better. Besides the obvious benefits of walking, such as improved cardiovascular fitness, maintaining a healthy weight, losing body fat, and preventing or managing various conditions including heart disease, stroke, and high blood pressure, I get to enjoy the 54321 exercise as the highlight of my walks. I get to discover and see something new each time. Also, when I'm feeling wound up, I like to do this exercise as it's a practical way to calm anxiety by isolating each of my senses through observation. Using your senses is a great way to reconnect with your body when you feel overwhelmed, have difficulty concentrating, or feel anxious.

We carry with us five senses – touch, taste, smell, hearing, and sight – but we often register those sensations unconsciously. Using these tools, we can become aware, accepting, and mindful of the external world. We can only see, smell, touch, taste, and hear in the present. I talk a lot about being outdoors, but this is an exercise you can do even indoors because it's simply you noticing your environment using your senses. We take our senses with us everywhere we go; therefore the 54321 exercise has limitless possibilities.

The 54321 exercise incorporates our five senses while allowing us a purposeful pause, making us mindful of our environment and creating a healthy sense of being in the moment:

1. **Sight**: Look around you and name **five** different objects.

2. **Hear**: Close your eyes and listen for **four** different sounds; birds, computer humming, kids playing, sirens, etc.

3. **Feel/Touch**: Look at, name, and touch **three** different objects, noticing their texture, temperature, mass, and weight as you do so.

4. **Smell**: Close your eyes and smell **two** different aromas, such as hand lotion, coffee, or outdoors after the first rain.

5. **Taste**: slowly enjoy a bite or sip of **one** thing of your choice and savor it, slowly. Experience the taste, texture, temperature, and any feelings you experience as you chew and swallow.

Notice the physical sensations throughout your body – sights, smells, sounds, tastes, touch/sensations. What did that feel like?

_____

_____

_____

_____

_____

What was the biggest surprise you felt?

_____

_____

_____

_____

Body Scan Exercise

The purpose of this exercise is to simply notice your body. It is not necessarily about relaxing your body; however, this may be a result. Usually, our response to bodily pain or discomfort is to distract ourselves or to try and numb the pain.

In this exercise, you will accept and notice with gentle curiosity your body in its comfort and discomfort. Sit or lie down in a comfortable position, making sure that you do not have any constrictions. Loosen any tight clothing. Starting with your feet, pay attention to the physical feelings in them: any pain, discomfort, coolness, warmth, tension, tightness, whatever. Simply pay attention to the physical feelings and sensations. Don't judge them as good or bad, don't try to change them, just be aware of them.

Slowly allow your awareness to drift up from your feet to your lower legs, again simply paying attention to any physical sensations in that part of your body, including any tightness, pain, or discomfort. Then slowly let your awareness drift further up your body, doing the same gentle noticing for all the parts of your body – your upper legs, hips, buttocks, pelvic region, stomach, chest, lower back, upper back, fingers, and hands, lower arms, upper arms, shoulders, neck, your head, forehead, temples, face – eyes, cheeks, nose, mouth, jawline.

Next, let your awareness drift gently and slowly back down your body, noticing any other places where there is pain, discomfort, or tension and simply noticing this until your awareness settles back at your feet.

Do this exercise for just five minutes. Just allow yourself to pay attention to the sensations in your body. If, while doing this exercise, thoughts intrude, that's okay – just notice the thoughts, notice yourself noticing those thoughts and gently guide your awareness back to your body. This is not about making yourself wrong, this is about just being and being ok with that.

Mindful Breathing

Become aware of your body and the places where it meets something solid: your feet on the floor, perhaps the backs of your legs against the chair... your thighs, buttocks, back, maybe shoulders resting where gravity lands them.

Notice where your hands touch - each other, or your body - notice the fabric of your clothes on your skin, and maybe the air on your skin. Notice your head resting on your shoulders and your arms hanging from your shoulders.

Let your senses move to the sounds around you, not needing to think about them, but just letting your attention move from sound to sound. Perhaps you can detect some odors, or a taste in your mouth, let yourself simply notice them.

Leave all of that now to focus on your breath, your simple natural breath. Bring all your attention to the breath as it moves in and out of your body, so the only movement you are aware of is the movement that is caused by your breath; in and out. Notice it wherever it is easiest to detect it. In and out of your nostrils or mouth, cool air in and warm air out, or at your chest or abdomen, rising and falling.

As thoughts arise, as they inevitably will, simply notice them and let them move on. No need to chase after them. Just bring your attention back again to your breath, your normal, natural breath, as it moves in and out of your body.

You have nowhere else to be, nothing else to do. Simply notice with gentleness and non-judgment of your breath. Practice this for a moment.

Now, expand your awareness outside of your body, to the sounds around you, to whatever feelings you have in your body. Notice any changes, any tensions, tightness, or looseness. Experience the world around you as you feel your body again in the chair or on the cushion and open your eyes when you are ready to return to this space.

What did you notice? Were there any surprises you felt during this exercise?

_____

_____

_____

_____

_____

Mindful Eating

I have had a love affair with food. It provided comfort for me when I was younger, especially when I returned from being with my biological mother, Cookie. I also had internalized feelings of shame and guilt about my affliction with food and my chubby physique, due to the teasing and put-downs I experienced from Cookie. I ate my food very quickly; I would eat to feel satisfied. I was obviously overeating because I wasn't allowing my body to sense that it was full and satisfied, resulting in my constant overeating. I would eat like this well into my adulthood despite the warnings I received. My maternal uncle was a trailblazing fitness guru in the Bay Area. My uncle, Billy E. Jones, founder of Jones-er-cize, would often talk to me about eating slower. I didn't know it then, but my uncle was teaching me to eat mindfully. Mindful eating can help in your weight loss and fitness goals which is a future outcome, but truthfully in the moment, you get to experience everything that piece of food has to offer.

You can practice this exercise with anything that you want. Variety is the spice of life so don't limit yourself. Try a raisin, a piece of chocolate, a piece of fruit, or a muffin on a plate. Before you choose one, come to a place of mindfulness. Sense what your body needs. Notice whether saliva production increases as you look at the plate. Take your time to choose one thing.

Focus with clear awareness on each movement and each moment of the experience as you move your arm, hand, and fingers towards the object and pick it up, place it on the palm of your hand, or hold it between your fingers.

Imagine you are new to Earth and have just come across this new substance you have not encountered before. Explore it with all your senses as if you have never seen it before. Scan it and explore every part of it with your eyes as it sits on your palm or in your fingers. Turn it around. Notice the texture, the light on it, its shape, whether it is soft, hard, coarse, or smooth. Notice any thoughts that arise (like "Why am I doing this?") and see if you can just acknowledge the thoughts and let them be before bringing your awareness back to the object.

Place the object beneath your nose and carefully notice the smell of it. Bring the object to one ear and squeeze it, roll it, and listen for any sound coming from it. Begin to slowly take the object into your mouth, noticing that the arm knows exactly where to go. Perhaps you're noticing your mouth watering in anticipation. Gently place the food in your mouth or take one bite if it is larger than bite-sized, but do not chew yet. Feel it on your tongue: its weight, temperature, size, and texture. Explore the sensations of it in your mouth.

When you are ready, intentionally bite into it. Does it go automatically to one side of the mouth? Notice when the flavors release. Slowly, slowly chew, noticing the change in consistency, until you are conscious of the impulse to swallow. Sense the food moving down to your throat and into your esophagus on its way to your stomach. Sit with the experience, noticing any vestiges remaining in your mouth, on your tongue, any flavors, and feelings you experience such as satisfaction, pleasure, or aversion. Take a moment to congratulate yourself for taking the time to experience mindful eating.

Meditation

Yoga, sitting meditation, and walking meditation are all forms of meditation. Learning a meditation practice takes practice and it's often not what most people think. It's about being present with yourself in that moment. You will discover that there is both pleasure and power in being present—you'll directly attend to and investigate how your experiences create such reactions as pleasure or discomfort in the mind and body.

Some people think it's difficult to meditate. Some think that they aren't doing it right because they can't stop their intrusive thoughts. Some imagine that while meditating, they will be so calm and peaceful that they will levitate. Let me break it down: your mind will always have intrusive thoughts. Our brains will never stop thinking about things. In meditation, the goal is to simply notice those thoughts and gently guide yourself back to your breathing, or your focal point. It may seem like your entire mediation session is you bringing your attention back and that is what the goal is. In my private practice, many of my clients have high-functioning anxiety, which is someone who experiences anxiety while still managing daily life quite well. Generally, a person with high-functioning anxiety may appear put together and well-accomplished on the outside, yet experience worry, and stress or have obsessive thoughts on the inside. Mediation has helped my clients tremendously.

There is evidence from research that shows that mindfulness meditation can lower stress, protectively change the brain, and help you sleep better, among other benefits. It makes me feel great and I find it easy to fit it into my daily routine. I usually choose a mindfulness meditation from the app Calm or YouTube. I have found that I enjoy having someone guide me in my practice. On YouTube, I like the 10-15 minute or 20-30-minute mindfulness meditation videos depending on how much time I allocate for the day.

Notice I said, "how much time I allocate for the day" instead of, "how much time I have", as I have the power to choose what I spend my time on each day. Some like just listening to music or nature sounds, and some prefer silence. I suggest trying them all out to see which one you like the best. Like anything, the more you practice, the better you get at it and the easier it becomes. Additionally, you may start craving it because you can feel the results and benefits that it has on your daily mood and feelings about yourself and others.

If you've ever practiced yoga, then you experienced meditation. When you practice body scans and deep breathing exercises, you are practicing a form of meditation. There are so many apps that can also help with your practice. As I mentioned above, Calm is my favorite. If you're a member of Kaiser Permanente, you are eligible to receive the premium services for free. Headspace is another one that teaches you how to meditate.

I love that there's a growing awareness in the African American community and we are incorporating it into our self-care and daily routines. It is also creating businesses. Women are hosting retreats and meditations are part of the agenda and activities. Black Women Healing is a prime example of a thriving business dedicated to Black women providing them an experience centered around mindfulness. I have never personally experienced their lovely events due to their age restrictions; however, they have created an environment to foster centeredness and stillness.

Deep Breathing Exercises

I believe this is my absolute favorite mindfulness technique. Baby, when I tell you I need deep breathing in my life. Not a day goes by now that I don't deep breathe. It feels so cleansing. When I am feeling stressed, I deep breathe, when I'm feeling anxious and worried, I deep breathe, when I feel agitated and frustrated, I deep breathe, when I feel pissed and angry, I deep breathe, and when I feel upset and overwhelmed, I deep breathe. When I'm feeling scared or nervous, I take deep breaths just to give myself a lift. It's my go-to when I need to regulate myself. I didn't start deep breathing until my early forties. When I say I could have used this 30 years ago, I am so serious! It could have prevented some of those cases I caught, especially when I threw hot chocolate at the restaurant owner, or when I destroyed the house because I was in a fit of rage, when I was road raging, or getting hyphy when things didn't go my way. I used to get *angry*. I would do this Incredible Hulk, puffed-up breathing thing. I'm telling you, it was a sight to see and it was the opposite of deep breathing. This shallow, hyperventilating type of breathing resulted in my becoming even more upset and dysregulated. I promise you that deep breathing will become your go-to in almost any scenario when you need to just "woosah".

For the sake of this exercise, the deep breathing you'll try now is to simply notice, accept, and be aware of your breath – it is not about relaxation or stress reduction, although this may also occur.

Breathing is something we all do – if you have a pulse then you're breathing. Your body knows how to do this; it has done it since birth. This is simply about breathing mindfully. Breathing is something you carry with you everywhere; you are just not usually aware of it. There is something uniquely different from when we are just breathing versus when we are intentionally paying attention to our breath throughout the practice of deep breathing. When we stop and take deep deliberate breaths it resets us, even if it is during a stressful situation. The body cannot remain in a heightened arousal state when you do deep breathing exercises. It's biologically and scientifically impossible. Look at that! You have your very own 'CONTROL ALT DEL' function to reset yourself.

Over the years I have learned the benefits of deep breathing and I have adapted a few methods that I continue to use with my clients. The first technique I like to call *double-ups*. I call it this because you first inhale for a few seconds, hold, and exhale double what you inhaled. You can use the counting ratio of 3/1/6 or 4/1/8. If you really want to make it deliberate, try 5/1/10 or 6/1/12. I recommend visualizing all of what you want in your life as you inhale and everything you don't want, release, and surrender it as you exhale. For example, if you want peace, joy, abundance, and love, visualize those things as you inhale. Another variation of this is called the Box method. You inhale four seconds, hold four seconds, exhale for four seconds, and pause for four seconds.

In my private practice, I teach every client this technique. Often during our session, we will do deep breathing, as I may need to help a client regulate themselves during the session. Another method is the STAR Method. I use this method frequently when working with children. It uses your ability to focus on a focal point. As the name implies, you visualize a star, start at the top point, and inhale and exhale as you move down and around each point of the star until you make it back to the top. I like using this version too because I have a 'monkey brain' that likes to jump around from thought to thought and it anchors my thinking so that I can focus on my breath.

It's your turn to try one of these methods out. Let's try it out now.

What technique did you try and why?

_____

_____

_____

_____

What was the sensation you felt afterward?

_____

_____

_____

_____

Would you try it again?

_____

_____

Will you try another technique next time? Why or why not?

_____

_____

_____

You will start to notice that each time you breathe in, your diaphragm or abdomen will expand, and each time you breathe out your diaphragm or abdomen will relax. Again, don't try to do anything – just be aware of the physical sensations of breathing in and breathing out. If you find that thoughts intrude, this is okay. Don't worry, just recognize the thoughts, allow them to be, and gently bring your awareness back to your breath.

Start this exercise initially for three minutes, building up daily. You can also do this exercise lying down in bed if you have difficulty sleeping. It is simply a way of allowing yourself to have a more mindful and conscious awareness of your body and its surroundings, its breathing, and its capacity to relax. When our breathing relaxes, our muscles relax, and as a result we are relaxed.

Practice Daily Breathing Exercises, Five Deep Breaths Twice a Day

Mindfulness is most effective when it is a lifetime commitment. I challenge you to explore the many ways that you can integrate mindfulness more fully and personally into your life. While having a dedicated regular practice of mindfulness meditation is important and beneficial, it is just as important to bring a broader sense of awareness and presence to every moment in your life and to use non-judgmental mindfulness in your self-reflection and decision-making processes. You'll learn how to maintain the discipline and flexibility of daily practice as circumstances change throughout your life. This is a tool you can take with you anywhere you go, and you can pull it out any time you want. Some examples may include sitting in bumper-to-bumper traffic, while you're on the phone with an unhelpful customer service agent, while you're standing in the express line at the grocery store behind someone who clearly has double the maximum items, or during that intense conversation with your spouse about helping with the house or kids. The possibilities are limitless because life gives us many opportunities to practice emotional intelligence, and deep breathing is the keystone to that. You have to realign yourself to make reasonable choices and decisions. Deep breathing will help you do that. In reflection, ask yourself:

How do I see my breath connected to my life?

_____

_____

_____

Why is incorporating mindfulness in my life important?

_____

_____

_____

_____

_____

What can I put in place to make space for my daily breathing exercises?

_____

_____

_____

_____

_____

EMPOWER

CHAPTER 4

Positive Affirmations - Loving Yourself

In Chapter 2 you learned all about those pesky ANTs aka cognitive distortions, so you know they can color your viewpoint. The way we see the world, ourselves, and others, is based on our attitudes and beliefs. If our attitude, philosophy, beliefs, and thoughts are generally negative, then our worldview can be very daunting and doom-and-gloom as well. Our beliefs and attitudes impact everything in our lives, from our health to our careers, family, relationships, and more. Our negative attitude can have a fulfilling prophecy effect and pull us into a downward spiral of negative thinking and living.

Fortunately for us, we can equate our brain to a powerful muscle that can be trained and retrained to have positive thoughts and beliefs. I don't know about you, but I find that information transformative. Let that sink in again. We have the power to slowly retrain our brains to think positively! By simply implementing these simple techniques you too will be on your way to positive THINKING, positive FEELING, and positive LIVING!

Brag Bag, You Better Work!

We all have been inundated with negative messages during your lives and they have shaped the way we think about ourselves. These messages come from our childhood, traumatic experiences, societal messages, gender and racial messages, news media, social media, music, art, and so on. It's time for you to reprogram yourself. Every day say a positive affirmation and each week add a new one. We have to say kind things to ourselves. We have to say powerful things to ourselves. They will manifest. Words have powerful vibrations to shift and create things. It starts with you SAYING It. You then will BELIEVE it and then you will ACT like it.

We all possess unique qualities. Sometimes we can see our greatness and sometimes we cannot. It takes practice. This is not about you being conceited or cocky. This is about re-affirming your superpower, the power of *you*. There is no one like you. You were uniquely created.

I watched an interview with one of my favorite artists, the Queen of Hip-Hop Soul, Mary J. Blige. She spoke about a time when she met her favorite artist, Chaka Khan, and Chaka gave her some advice. "You are incredible, but you need to get out of your own way." Mary said she didn't know what that meant back then but she does now. Mary goes on to say, "It means don't be afraid of your gift, don't be afraid of yourself, don't be afraid of the power and the gift that you're going to give to people, don't hate on yourself, don't speak negatively about yourself, don't be your own worst enemy. It's about just having the courage and knowing who you are, knowing yourself as much as you can."

Many of us walk around downplaying our gifts and talents. At times your superpower is evident and other times it's in our blind spot. Remember, we are taking the inner critic out of the dialogue. This is building your inner wellness and strengthening that muscle. It takes practice, daily practice, and intentional practice.

Previously I mentioned how our language matters, and what and how you say it matters. You can speak life or death into your world. Many years ago, while I worked with a life coach, she highlighted to me how I spoke and described scenarios and desired outcomes. I kept saying, "I don't want to (fill in the blank), I don't want (fill in the blank), I don't want to deal with (fill in the blank), I don't have (fill in the blank)." She encouraged me to replace what I didn't want with what I did want and to speak in the present as if I already had it. It's called the Law of Attraction. Whatever you focus your energy on will expand. By focusing on what you want to achieve, be, or have, the law states that you'll emit positive energy to attract those desires to you. When speaking, affirm with:

I am _____

I do _____

I have _____

Are You Ready to Get into Action?

Spend some intentional time and effort and use the area below to list your strengths, positive skills, qualities, abilities, and achievements together with an illustration or evidence that demonstrates or supports the affirmation. Once you have completed the exercise, read through your list daily to confirm how badass you are. Later in this workbook, you'll have time to revisit this list and intentionally access these affirmations to position yourself for the *Glow Up.*

Fill in the "Illustration or Supporting Evidence" column, where applicable, and give an example of when you demonstrated the positive characteristic or your other reasons for believing that you have that quality. Completing this exercise is affirming for you and makes it plain for you that there is a solid basis for the belief expressed in your affirmation.

Affirmation of Strength, Skill, Quality, Ability or Achievement	Illustration or Supporting Evidence (complete where applicable)

How was that exercise for you? Any surprises? How are you feeling as you reflect on your answers?

_____

_____

_____

_____

_____

Yum Your Yuck

Your beliefs and how you talk to yourself can either empower you or hold you back. How do you think your beliefs are serving you?

Our mindset is <u>everything.</u> We as human beings tend to get stuck in ruts or feed off others' negative energy or attitude, AND yet we still have the power of choice. I attended a training once and one of the ground rules was "don't yuck my yum" which basically meant *don't hate on someone else's thoughts and ideas*. We are 'hatin' on ourselves a majority of the time. We do it in very small ways, ways we don't really pay attention to but trust me, it is having an effect. Have you ever been driving, kind of on autopilot, and you miss your exit and the first thing you say is 'aw shit, what the hell is wrong with me?" Or "I'm such a space cadet!" Since I have attention deficit disorder (ADD), I've jokingly called myself a space cadet but that's not cool. We unconsciously talk badly to ourselves. It's a sneaky way we put ourselves down.

Self-deprecation is an unhealthy way of criticizing ourselves with humor and fun. It's fine to laugh at yourself; however, criticizing is a slippery slope. The purpose of the positive affirmation principle in the EMPOWER framework is for you to shift your mindset to see yourself in a positive light and practice replacing the negative with positive self-talk. This is experienced as positive self-concept, positive self-esteem, and positive self-acceptance. Even in moments where you made an error, you are OK, you are *enough*, you are *worth it*, and you are *loved*. (You are kind, you are smart, you are important.) Thank you, Viola Davis, for the reminder.

Here is a list of positive thoughts. To help with this practice I use the app called I AM. It peppers me with positive vibes all day. When the notification comes up, I don't swipe it off like a pesky notification; I stop and read it. It only takes a few seconds, and the benefits are long-lasting. It's like after you leave the gym, you still are getting the benefits afterward and all day. Your metabolism is still working, and positive affirmations are just as powerful. It strengthens your mental and emotional intelligence muscles, which increases your sense of well-being.

One of my favorite TV shows was *Insecure*. Each week I couldn't wait to see what Essa Rae and her crew were up to. I believe one of the reasons I loved the show so much was because I resonated with Essa and her inner chatter. As a Black woman, even as an educated Black woman, I still felt inadequate and unsure of myself. But the highlight and most enjoyable parts (outside of the sex scenes, don't judge me) were her mirror self-talks and rap bars, especially when she hyped herself up. We gotta be our own hype person. Here are several of my favorites from the I AM app:

"I am respected by my peers."

"I have a good sense of humor."

"I'm excited about my future."

"I will be successful."

"I am successful."

"I'm fun to be with."

"I am in a great mood."

"There are many people who care about me."

"I'm proud of my accomplishments."

"I will finish what I start."

"I have many good qualities."

"I am comfortable with life."

"I have a good way with others."

"I am blessed."

"I have friends who support me."

"Life is exciting."

"I am proud of myself."

"I feel good."

"No matter what happens, I know I'll make it."

"I can accomplish anything."

"I feel on point."

"Every day is a new day; I am growing and changing for the better."

"I enjoy a challenge."

"My social life is great."

"There's nothing to worry about."

"I'm so relaxed."

"My life is running smoothly."

"I'm happy with the way I look."

"I take good care of myself."

"I deserve the best in life."

"Bad days are rare."

"I have many useful qualities."

"There is no problem that is hopeless."

"I won't give up."

"I state my opinions with confidence."

"My life keeps getting better."

"Today I've accomplished a lot."

"I feel empowered."

"I'm warm and comfortable."

"I feel confident I can do anything I set my mind to."

"I feel very happy."

"This is super!"

"I have everything that I need."

Which affirmations resonate with you?

_____

_____

_____

_____

_____

What positive thoughts are you committed to saying and feeling about yourself?

_____

_____

_____

_____

_____

What other affirmations can you think of?

_____

_____

_____

_____

_____

Which affirmation(s) do you want to increase or start feeling like?

_____

_____

_____

_____

For the most impactful EMPOWERING beliefs, write them on a Post-it and place them where you will see and read them daily. Gabrielle Union's character on *Being Mary Jane* gave us this great idea. Post that shit everywhere! In the bathroom, in the kitchen, in the bedroom, on the way out the door, in your workspace, hell, I even had a Post-It on my car's dashboard.

We can choose to think thoughts that make us feel good or we can choose to think thoughts that have us feeling like our lives are terrible or mediocre. We can also look and see that there are areas we can stretch ourselves into. It's a matter of mindset.

Balancing Statements for Negative Self-Talk

Here is where we switch gears a bit. As I discussed earlier, we are prone to think negatively. That's just how the brain is wired. These beliefs are mostly faulty and do not serve us but awareness is everything. I want you to make a list. I want you to think of the beliefs that limit you or discourage you and write those down in the left-hand column. In the right column write down an alternative statement that balances the first statement by moderating it realistically. See the example below and feel free to do it in the manner that feels the most useful. Remember the 4vP Formula from Chapter 1.

Negative Description of Self	Realistic Balancing Statement
Ex. "I always sabotage my life" (also indicate here the situation in which you applied this description to yourself)	"I overreacted on this occasion. However, last week I managed to detach myself and relax more. I will try to do better next time."

Did you notice in the example, I used the word "always"? Remember that's a sneaky cognitive distortion. It's an overgeneralization. Nothing is ever 'always and never'. I work really hard at not using those words to describe something or someone's behaviors. In addition, I have to put my listening ears on when speaking with a person who uses those terms; instantly I want to check out because I'm like, 'Nope, you're on that BS'. However, everyone is not privy to how those words shape and limit their communication or hold that perspective so I will pause and attempt to hear the real message.

Let's Play the List of 3's

Okay Sis, you are working it now, you are recognizing your language and the conscious and unconscious ways you communicate. In this section, you'll get the opportunity to practice and flex this positive affirmation muscle a bit more.

Complete the following questions by answering them with a heart of kindness and imagination, then remind yourself how bomb you are when you are feeling a dip and whenever you need a boost. Commit to reading it daily.

List three positive characteristics you have.

1._____

2._____

3._____

List three things that you are proud of about yourself.

1._____

2._____

3._____

List three things you have achieved.

1._____

2._____

3._____

List three ways to treat yourself if you're feeling down or ways to reward yourself if you've done something well (refrain from listing money, food, or drugs).

1._____

2._____

3._____

List three things you can do to make yourself laugh.

1._____

2._____

3._____

List three things that you can do to help feel good about yourself.

1._____

2._____

3._____

Complete the sentence: Looking above makes me realize that I____

_____

_____

_____

_____

Confidence

Confidence helps us feel ready for life's experiences. When we're confident, we're more likely to move forward with people and opportunities, not back away from them. And if things don't work out at first, confidence helps us try again. Have you ever wondered why some have it and others don't? Do you wish you had more confidence?

Sis, you have the ability to increase your confidence. Did you know that good thoughts impact our confidence levels? People can learn to access confidence whenever they want or need to. We do it and don't realize that is what's going on. You might be talking about a future 10K race when you remember last year's race and how you trained and did your personal best; your family was there cheering you on, and you were so confident and empowered when you finished. Remembering past experiences will allow you to re-access the same emotions.

Confidence may show up in different areas of your life. Think of a time when you felt really confident. We all have felt confident at one time or another. You may be confident at work, you may be confident with your friends or maybe you're confident at a daily task like applying your make-up or putting together an outfit.

My confidence has wavered from time to time. I recall a time when my confidence was at sub-zero. I applied for a promotion, not once but three times, and was overlooked each time! I wondered what was wrong with me, I doubted my abilities, and I regretted applying because the rejection felt so painful. I remember crying and feeling so low and stuck. My imposter syndrome was in full throttle. I questioned myself thinking I wasn't qualified, and maybe they too thought I was not good enough. It required me to do some inner work to break that mindset. I wholeheartedly devoted myself to my own transformation, starting from the inside out.

Believe Everything Happens in Divine Timing

During this timeframe, my good friend Stacy Hogg invited me to a universally known, personal and professional development program called Landmark Worldwide that took place over the course of four days. The cost seemed steep at the time, but I trusted her and was open to the experience. Little did I know that those four days would change the course of my life. It was intense individual and group work with processing, sharing, and healing. The buried pain and shame from my mother's abandonment turned to empathy and compassion. I understood how my subconscious beliefs were holding me back, and I finally claimed the type of woman I wanted to be and the life I wanted to live.

I applied again for the Program Manager position when the opportunity came up again and I got the promotion. I started my private counseling practice, and soon after, my Success Mindset coaching business. I won the 'most transformed' award in a bodybuilding contest. The relationship with my mother healed, and the money flowed.

In reflection, I actually had much to be proud of, especially from where I came from. My setbacks and mistakes don't define me, they only enhanced my growth. In general, I have been an outgoing, and confident person with a lot of doubt. Yet, I am proud of the woman I'm becoming. My mindset has changed. My priorities have changed. My taste has changed. My tolerance has changed. I'm constantly evolving, and I'm 100 percent here for it.

What are you confident about?

_____

_____

_____

_____

Imagine you are confident right now. How does that feel in this moment?

_____

_____

_____

_____

As you remember feeling confident, you will start to feel confident. Think about this feeling, where in your body does this feeling of confidence start?

_____

_____

_____

_____

Imagine you can see your feeling of confidence. What color is it?

_____

_____

How can you make this feeling brighter and stronger?

_____

_____

_____

Positive Affirmations - Loving Yourself

How we talk to ourselves matters. The conversations going on in our heads are our thoughts. Have you ever had a thought that you can't seem to shake? Was it a negative thought? You are not alone; you are human and that's what we do. The mind is designed to navigate toward negative thoughts because it's a defense mechanism. Research says a person has over 70,000 thoughts a day and more than half are negative. Another mind-blowing fact is that approximately 90% of our thoughts are repetitive, so we are just regurgitating our thoughts. That's why it's so important to be intentional when retraining your brain. Using positive affirmations can be extremely helpful in shutting down your inner critic, boosting your confidence, and increasing your capacity for self-love. Remember that people can only love to the level of their self-love, they can only communicate to their own level of self-awareness, and they can only behave to their level of healed trauma.

The world tells us enough negative things. As a Black woman, I carry the burden of the dismissal of Black women and when Malcolm X said we are the least protected, I totally agree. That is why we have to love on *ourselves*. There are enough haters in the world, you don't need to add to the list. As MJB said, "Don't hate on yourself, don't speak negatively about yourself, don't be your own worst enemy."

To support our positive affirmation practice we will incorporate technology to help us out. As a society, we constantly rely on our smartphones. Fortunately for us, they are tools we can use to enhance our mood. ThinkUp is an app that I've been using for years. Both my mental health and coaching clients use it, and they have recognized that it is beneficial to their daily well-being. I use it every morning and it sets my daily intentions. There are hundreds to choose from. Download the app ThinkUp now and choose and record your four affirmations.

What are the four affirmations you chose?

_____

_____

_____

_____

Now ask yourself, "How can I make this a regular habit?"

_____

_____

_____

_____

_____

_____

What is one thing I am committed to doing to ensure my success in making this a habit?

_____

_____

_____

_____

Keep in mind that positive affirmation and self-talk may not get you there without other interventions such as therapy and self-reflection. However, it is a great start.

What Makes Your Heart Sing?

What makes your heart sing? What makes us happy is usually free, so why aren't we doing more of it? Why are we so busy chasing material goals? Instead, make time for enjoyable, rejuvenating, and satisfying activities like service organizations, sports, hobbies, and entertainment. Organize your work or business and other obligations *around* these commitments to fun because it has all sorts of health benefits. It gives you more energy.

When you are with others and enjoying yourself, there are bound to be moments of mirth and fun. Dancing, for instance, brings smiles to many faces – both participants and onlookers.

Don't be shy or worry about making a fool of yourself. Life is too short for such considerations. One of the health benefits of fun is that having fun gives you more energy to have even more fun. It relieves stress.

Doctors tell us that stress can do untold damage to our mental and physical health. Taking part in fun activities that relieve stress and take your mind off worries has health benefits. These activities may be sedentary, like playing board games, or more physical like walking or swimming. One of the health benefits of fun is that it boosts your serotonin levels. Higher serotonin is associated with improved sleep patterns and a more relaxed and positive outlook on life. Serotonin is a naturally occurring chemical that can affect your mood and emotions. Research indicates that a lack of serotonin can lead to poor sleep patterns, stress, or anxiety.

Play and other activities that don't have a purpose other than helping us feel relaxed and happy keep our minds focused on the present. The present is where joy lives. I don't know about you but I'm here for the joy, baby!

Allow yourself 10-15 minutes of quiet time and write your answers in the space below. Don't overthink, just write! If your answers seem too simple, good! In a notepad or journal keep adding to your list as things come to mind in the days and weeks ahead.

Think back as far as you can remember- what were you doing when you were most happy? Think about your five senses: sight, hearing, touch, smell, and taste. You could even come up with one per sense. A few of my joys are beaches, clear and warm days, sunsets, live music, old school R&B and hip hop, dancing, chocolate, ice cream, walking/hiking in nature, adult coloring books, lifting weights, and traveling.

Now it's your turn to answer this for yourself. What are the top ten joys in your life?
1.
2.
3.
4.
5.
6.
7.
8.
9.
10.

Identify three actions to bring more of the 'heart-sing' items into your life.
1.
2.
3.

Throughout this book, you will hear me repeat the phrase "the power of choice". You have the power to *choose* to do the things that make your heart sing *and* to be grateful.

I Choose to Be Grateful

Gratitude is the greatest gift we have. It is our source of power to overcome any obstacle and the strength within us to recognize we have what we need to manifest our happiness. Our mindset is based on how we *choose* to think.

I reflect on all that for which I'm grateful. I am most grateful for my mom who raised me. I am grateful for my mistakes and the tough experiences I have endured. I am grateful for my daughter. I am grateful for my friends and family support circle. I am grateful for my good health. I am grateful for my empathic tendencies, my infectious smile, with my flaws and all.

Like any emotion, gratitude can't be forced. However, we *can* cultivate our thoughts so that gratitude is more likely to arise. Practicing gratitude helps create a *habit* where we focus on the positive in life. We'll get into the longer version of this in a minute but first here's a quick way to get started on practicing gratitude.

Here's a tool called the "Five Things Gratitude" tool, or the "Do Anywhere Gratitude" exercise. Using your five fingers, or if you're feeling really full of gratitude, use all ten, list 5-10 people, places, or things you are grateful for. Let's start now!

I Am Committed and Will Enjoy My Journey

Practicing daily gratitude helps us in several ways. It kicks your version of "Listen, Linda" out of the way and stops ANTs from taking over. It's especially good for busy, and super busy women. Psst...YOU! It's important that you record your journey. You've already started that with some of the previous exercises.

We are going to take it up a notch with daily journaling. Some days you may not want to, and I get that. Don't be too hard on yourself if you miss a day here and there. I also encourage you to push through the emotion to skip and focus on what you will gain with the practice. I love journaling because I believe it is so powerful. Journaling evokes mindfulness and helps you remain present while keeping perspective. It presents an opportunity for emotional catharsis and helps the brain regulate emotions. It provides a greater sense of confidence and self-identity.

Each week you will add more practices to your daily routine. Journaling is imperative to your growth. The daily prompts are designed to help you recognize the small things we take for granted. If we choose, there is something to be grateful for every day we are living.

For the next four weeks, you will commit to answering three daily grateful prompts.

DAY 1

One good thing that happened to me today:

_____

_____

_____

_____

Something good that I saw someone do today:

_____

_____

_____

_____

Today I had fun when:

_____

_____

_____

_____

DAY 2

Something I accomplished today:

_____

_____

_____

_____

_____

Something funny that happened today:

_____

_____

_____

_____

_____

Someone I was thankful for today:

_____

_____

_____

_____

_____

DAY 3

Something I was thankful for today:

_____

_____

_____

_____

Today I smiled when:

_____

_____

_____

_____

Something about today I'll always want to remember:

_____

_____

_____

_____

_____

DAY 4

One good thing that happened to me today:

_____

_____

_____

_____

Today was a day special because:

_____

_____

_____

_____

Today I was proud of myself because:

_____

_____

_____

_____

DAY 5

Something interesting that happened today:

_____

_____

_____

_____

Someone I was thankful for today:

_____

_____

_____

_____

Today I had fun when:

_____

_____

_____

_____

DAY 6

Something about today I'll always want to remember:

_____

_____

_____

_____

_____

Something funny that happened:

_____

_____

_____

_____

_____

My favorite part of today:

_____

_____

_____

_____

_____

DAY 7

Something I was happy about today:

_____

_____

_____

_____

Something good I saw someone do today:

_____

_____

_____

_____

Something I did well today:

_____

_____

_____

_____

Rate your day, first day, gut score 1-10. In the end, do you see any difference in how you feel about your day?

_____

_____

_____

_____

After all, it's our thoughts about the day and not the day itself that affects how we feel.

EMPOWERed Reflection

What was the biggest surprise for you from this exercise?

_____

_____

_____

_____

_____

Which questions did you enjoy answering? Why?

_____

_____

_____

What learning could you take forward to tomorrow?

_____

_____

_____

_____

_____

Where could you benefit from being more positive/thankful/grateful in your life?

_____

_____

_____

_____

Do you notice that the day is a collection of different moments? You have the power of choice in how you summarize and think of your days. How will you choose?

By consciously choosing and repeating positive statements, we can reframe our self-perception, nurture self-compassion, and unlock our full potential. Through consistent practice and integration into our daily lives, positive affirmations can become a catalyst for personal growth, empowerment, and a deep sense of self-worth.

EMPOWER

CHAPTER 5

Own Your Story, Own Your Power - Honoring Yourself

Forgive The Past, Live in The Present

Forgiveness is a human capacity required to experience internal peace. When we forgive, we lay down our burdens of fear, hurt, and anger. On the journey of self-acceptance and massive growth, you must be willing to let things from the past go. You must be willing to forgive those who have hurt you. You must be willing to forgive yourself. The result of forgiveness is a clearing for our inner passages so we can receive more healing and inner peace. Some of us have experienced hurts from our childhood, others are from life experiences. Some of these hurts can cause lasting pain and resentment, often resulting in maladaptive ways of dealing with the discomfort. What is forgiveness and what does it mean to forgive? We often are resistant to forgiving someone because we feel like we are accepting their behavior, therefore we are giving them our power. However, when you release hurts, anger, disappointments, failures, and rejection from the past, you are helping yourself and reclaiming your power.

The irony about holding onto past hurts is that it's probably more on your mind and bothering you more than the perpetrator. This requires energy and space you just don't have time for! We also may hold on because we want them to acknowledge the hurt and give us an apology. Yet again, do you really need the person who hurt you to tell you, 'I hurt you and I'm sorry and I feel awful that I did it?' It's beautiful to get an apology, but do you *need* it? Do you not know how painful the pain was when you experienced it? Do you need them to tell you how painful it was and permit you to feel it?

You don't need it. The one who hurt you cannot heal you. *You* have to heal you. You can't expect the person who broke you into pieces to bring those pieces back together and say, "I'm going to fix you." So, at the end of the day, we don't need a person to validate what we are feeling to create the pathway to our healing. Forgiveness is for you, not them. You have the power, only you.

I suspect you got this book because you want to increase your joy and excitement and decrease the drain and sabotage in your life. It starts with you letting go of the baggage. We all know the words to Erykah Badu's song, *Bag Lady*. Sing it with me, ladies!

We may even think we have forgiven something from our past only to discover it's been festering inside of us. Forgiveness is transformative. Forgiveness is a step toward freeing yourself to enjoy life. You don't need to know *how* to let go, you just need to be *willing* to let go. It starts with the mindset and soon the behavior will follow.

My forgiveness journey started with the resentment I felt towards my biological mother. For years I hated that she picked drugs over my siblings and me. I felt she was selfish to live her lifestyle knowing she had four children and didn't raise any of us. I resented her because I felt she robbed me of the ability to be raised with my siblings. I also walked around with shame because I knew my mother lived a life of prostitution and drug addiction. Sure, there were others in my community and circle who had parents on crack, but it was still embarrassing as fuck. I also had animosity toward my biological father. I blamed him for exploiting my mother when she was a child and for the ongoing abuse and manipulation she endured. It wasn't until much later I made the connections between the absence of my father in my life, with his known profession as a pimp that shaped my perception and influenced my choices in men. I later learned my paternal great-grandmother was a madam and my father was raised in that environment.

Life continues to give us opportunities to forgive because people are people, so best believe somebody will do something that requires forgiveness. Another person I had to come to terms with in terms of forgiveness was my maternal grandmother. I have prided myself on not being a person who holds on to grudges but she was one I was not willing to release for years; however, I finally released them within the last five years. I resented my grandmother, or 'Big Mama', which was what she insisted on us calling her. But in reality (my reality), she did not care for her daughter's children, let alone her only daughter. She allowed us to be separated, and she did not attempt to get us, or even visit us. I remember her befriending my mama who raised me, and they would talk on the phone chatting it up about what teenage shenanigans I was into. It really rubbed me that she and my mama talked about me, and I felt she was just being nosey and did not have genuine care for me. I remember her being mean towards my mother Cookie and her showing favoritism towards her sons and her husband's children. My mother was the outcast. Cookie said she never understood why her mother was so mean to her. Even to this day, she is not kind to Cookie when she tries to call and check on her. My memories also included her saying hurtful things to me like "You're gonna be just like your mother." She was certainly throwing shade at me and putting me down. I later learned that my grandmother was repeatedly brutally beaten as a child and her mother abandoned her at a young age. Hurt people, hurt people.

There are other transgressions I've experienced, like the boy that raped me when I was 13, the mental, emotional, and physical abuse from boyfriends and husbands, the betrayals, the affairs, making kids outside of the marriage, being beaten up by the police, and financial abuse of my adoptive mother by an extended family member, just to name a few. Forgiveness of the past is a must. We cannot undo what happened to us. We cannot turn back the hands of time. We can only live in the present. Forgiveness releases us from the heavy burden of holding on to it. Forgiveness gives us our power back. Nelson Mandela said, "Forgiveness liberates the soul, that's why it is such a powerful weapon."

Again, we do not require an apology or acknowledgment or need someone to tell us how we feel or how we are impacted by their actions. There are three things that you need to come to terms with in life: one, if they wanted to, they would; two, no response is a response, and lastly, not everybody has the same values, the same goals, awareness, or the same heart that you do.

In this exercise, list the things you want to let go of and reflect on the benefits of doing that. I can understand if you are reluctant to do any of this right now. However, I encourage you to dig deep and start on your list. Just writing it out and making your list starts the process of your awareness of what's been in your heart, subconsciously in your mind, and being played out in subtle and overt ways. So, simply list what you're holding onto, what is slowing you down, keeping you stuck, and scared, what riles you up, and anything that gets in the way of you being your best self.

What do I need to let go of?

_____

_____

_____

_____

_____

_____

How do I benefit by 'holding on'?

_____

_____

_____

_____

_____

_____

_____

Now take a moment and imagine letting go of everything on your list. How does that feel?

_____

_____

_____

_____

_____

_____

What have you learned about yourself by doing this exercise?

_____

_____

_____

_____

_____

_____

Forgiving Others

Write it down. Make a list of all the people who have hurt you, no matter how small or large. Go back to childhood. After that, place the names in order from the lowest level of wrongdoing/violation and anger/hurt to the highest.

Reflect. Acknowledge the pain that your lack of forgiveness has caused you and how it currently impacts your life. Is it more painful than the actual experience? You'll start the process of forgiveness with someone toward the bottom of the list. This makes you comfortable with using your forgiving muscle. As you go up the list, it will become increasingly easier for you to forgive. You will experience the lightness and freedom you feel from the release.

Learn the lesson. What did you learn from this exercise?

_____

_____

_____

_____

_____

_____

Express forgiveness. If you feel this will be beneficial, go for it. There are several forms of communication so don't get hung up on the method. Remember this is for *you*, not for them. How was that for you?

_____

_____

_____

_____

_____

_____

_____

Free yourself. Forgiveness is about *owning your power*. This is an opportunity to grow, learn, and heal. This isn't about getting back at them, forging revenge, or holding that grudge. Forgiveness is about your peace so you can have freedom and joy.

Do you know the benefits of holding on to the grudge? There must be something or you wouldn't be holding on to it, so ask yourself, "What do I gain by keeping hold of this?" In some situations, perhaps by holding on to resentments, anger, and hurt, you don't need to accept your part in the situation, or perhaps it stops you from feeling how hurt you really were. Maybe you get to stay in the 'right' or avoid dealing with a difficult issue.

We also must let go of things we've done in the past. This can be hard, as we are often harder on ourselves than on others. I challenge you to ask yourself, "What do I need to do that will allow me to let this go?"

_____

_____

_____

_____

_____

This is an opportunity to write something you learned, or maybe this will be when you make some type of amendment, apology, or find a meaningful way for you to make up with someone or yourself.

While we cannot change the past, we can make amends and learn from it while living life to the fullest. Take a moment to reflect on your actions (toward yourself or others) in the past that you may regret. Are there any mistakes you've made that you continue to beat yourself up for? If so, what?

_____

_____

_____

_____

_____

How are you punishing yourself for these past mistakes?

_____

_____

_____

_____

_____

Are you directly or indirectly punishing others for them? If so, how?

_____

_____

_____

_____

_____

_____

Your guilt is not going to undo what has happened in the past. Even more importantly, holding onto this pain is causing further pain in your life. It is okay to let it go now. Forgiveness is not about you forgetting what happened. It's about how you react to those memories and the subconscious way they show up in your life. It is time for you to release yourself from the burden of carrying it with you. This also goes back to the impact of our thoughts on our health. Practicing forgiveness can have powerful health benefits. Observational studies, and even some randomized trials, suggest that forgiveness is associated with lower levels of depression, anxiety, hostility reduced substance abuse, higher self-esteem, and greater life satisfaction.

(https://www.health.harvard.edu/mind-and-mood/the-power-of-forgiveness). Own your power!

I forgive myself for:

_____

_____

_____

_____

_____

_____

Remember, forgiveness is a personal choice. Forgiveness is for your freedom and happiness. It's for you to learn, grow, and heal and you will be able to find that all experiences are blessings. Some are harder to recognize than others. Lastly, forgiveness is 100% *your* responsibility,

Identify Past Failures and Mistakes and The Lessons Learned

Regrets are reflections from the past and it is a mindset to regret something. Most of the time we associate the word *regret* as negative because we align it with a perceived missed opportunity, or the consequences of the decision are unfavorable. You might find yourself saying things like "I wish I didn't do XYZ" or "I should have done XYZ." I call it the "Could've, should've, would'ves". The next exercise is designed to help you come to terms with actions you feel bad about which, when you look at them in the context of the world's worries, really aren't that bad! And, even if it was 'bad', what is the lesson learned? Therefore, is it really *bad* since it's an opportunity to learn?

Boy oh boy, I could go down a rabbit hole if I wanted to reflect on all my "regrets". I should've gone to college immediately instead of waiting three years after high school, I should've gone to an HBCU instead of a PWI, I should've told someone when I got raped, I shouldn't have driven drunk which resulted in a DUI, I shouldn't have broken the law, repeatedly, I should've controlled my anger, I should've saved more money, I should've left unhealthy and abusive relationships at the first, second, third red flag, I should've resigned from my job years ago, I should've had more kids, I should've studied abroad. The list could be longer, but I've gotten over all these 'should'ves', I've *learned* from these 'should'ves'. Some lessons had to be repeated because I didn't take heed of the lessons immediately and all are a matter of acceptance and surrendering to the outcome. All in all, I had to shift the way I felt about my "regrets". I learned the power of giving myself grace and seeing the positive in every circumstance. I had to accept that I am always in the perfect place at the right time.

If you find yourself thinking 'I should have done X' or 'I should have not done Y', instead think of constructive/positive thoughts that you can tell yourself. Using constructive thoughts in place of negative thoughts helps you realize it may not be as bad as it looks, or that you may not be to blame as much as you think. Here are some alternative thoughts:

- There are positives which could be taken from the situation.

- I'll do something different next time.

- What happened is not entirely my fault.

- At least I did *something*! I did my best.

- Maybe the other person's reaction had nothing to do with what I did but had more to do with something else they were worried about at the moment or with their attitude.

- Am I jumping to conclusions?

What are some other considerations for those pesky regrets?

1._____

2._____

3._____

Next, I want you to think of two situations you have recently experienced where you thought that you should have done something differently. Then, complete the table, specifying in the left-hand column what you said to yourself (e.g. 'I should have done X…). In the right-hand column, think of an alternative thought you can replace the negative thought with to create a more balanced, constructive, self-compassionate approach.

DESCRIBE YOUR REGRET	ALTERNATIVE REPLACEMENT THOUGHT
❖	❖
❖	❖
❖	❖
❖	❖

Mistakes are all about mindset. Next time ask yourself these questions:

- What did I learn from the mistake?

- Did I know this information before?

- What problems were created when the *mistakes* were made?

- Have I corrected the problem?

- Would I forgive someone else who made the same *mistake*?

- Will I forgive yourself?

I am shedding who I was, embracing who I am, and admiring the woman I will become.

Miraculous Mistake

Mistakes are necessary for our learning. I call them miraculous because of the great possibilities, feedback, and knowledge they can offer. Scientists learn from making mistakes. The more mistakes they make, the more likely they are to achieve their goals. I'd like to challenge you to think of your life a bit that way. Life is a beta test; keep trying at it.

Think of five events in your life when you made a *mistake* and learned something from it.

MISTAKE	WHAT I LEARNED
❖	❖
❖	❖
❖	❖
❖	❖
❖	❖

Sometimes we need reminders that learning from our *mistakes* is growth. We need to be encouraged by our mistakes and not feel defeated.

Identification of the Most Valued Quality of Self and Others

Ask yourself "What do I like about *me*?" We all have strengths, gifts, skills, qualities, and personal preferences but the magic to life is understanding what you are good at and what you appreciate about yourself. I'm sure you may even feel like there are some things you are weak in or not as skilled in, but others think you do a good job or think it's a strength.

As we grow older, we sometimes forget the person we used to be, the young you before the worries and burdens of the world took hold. When we were younger, we often looked at things differently for several reasons. For starters, our brain isn't all the way developed so our perception of things and our decision making is much different from our 15-year-old self compared to our 25 or even our 35, 50, or 60-year-old selves.

Humor me for a minute and think back to when you were a teenager, what were you good at? What were your strengths? What did you love doing? What would other people, your friends, and peers say that they liked about you? What would others say were your strengths and qualities? I get it, it's hard to recognize these things in ourselves, partly because we've been socialized to avoid the spotlight and attention. *Don't think so highly of yourself, be modest, be humble.* I can appreciate being humble because it:

- Allows you to learn.

- It proves you don't know it all.

- It creates endless possibilities.

- It magnifies your strengths.

- It helps others connect with and relate to you.

- It keeps power in check.

- Humility empowers others to lead.

- It leads to curiosity.

Leading with humility does not shrink the confidence meter. It actually opens it up for your confidence to increase because of the aforementioned benefits.

What do you like about yourself?

_____

_____

_____

_____

_____

What Makes You Shine?

How do you shine? What gives you character? How are you a gem? The purpose of this exercise is to help you appreciate yourself just a little bit more - in all your uniqueness and differences! While we are all more similar than we realize, it helps us truly value ourselves when we recognize what makes us unique. For this exercise set aside 30 minutes to celebrate you! Find somewhere relaxing where you can sink into this exercise. Start by brainstorming your unique qualities, knowledge, skills, and experiences below. Some tips:

- No judgment, please. There is no "good" or "bad" here, there is just the reality of you.

- Think broadly, loosely, and from the heart.

- Include duplicates and similar items - these are good as they show a theme or pattern!

- Include small things, big things, and important and "unimportant" things.

- Include what makes you different, and unique-anything and everything that makes you *you*.

- Remember, this isn't about what looks good to others, but what *you* are proud of in yourself.

_____

_____

_____

_____

_____

_____

_____

_____

_____

When the area is filled, circle the ten items you're most proud of. For each ten things you circled, consider what strengths and qualities lie underneath. For example, completing a marathon might represent determination and *focus*. Leaving an unhealthy relationship might represent *courage*. Write these extra qualities next to them. Next, choose the *one* item you like most about yourself and put a star next to it.

What have I learned from this exercise?

_____

_____

_____

_____

_____

_____

What new belief could I now create about myself and carry forward in life?

_____

_____

_____

_____

_____

Control -Who Has It?

When owning your story and power, one of the most important things to do is to focus on the things that you can control. Too often we waste time and energy on things that are outside of our control and influence when we could be spending it on that abundant life we really want and already have. This is why many people never create their own stories; they are too focused on changing the wrong things. We need to direct our focus on things we *can* control, things within our "Circle of Control".

There are three levels of influence:

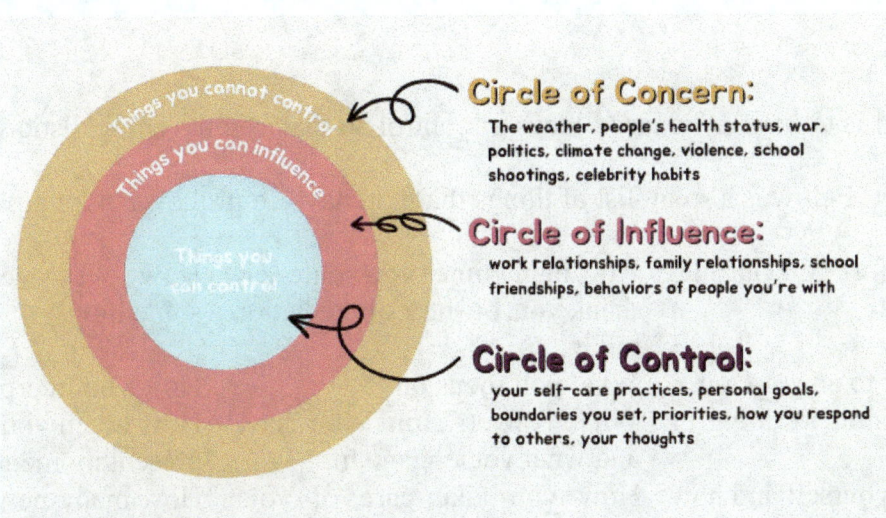

- Things that you can directly control.

- Things you can influence.

- Things that you have no control nor influence over.

So, let's take a deep dive. It's important to recognize that our perception of what we *can* control strongly influences what we do and what we feel about situations in our lives. The perception of how much control you have in your life is called "locus of control."

A person who has a *predominant internal locus of control* believes that they can (or should be able to) influence all the events and outcomes in their life. On the other hand, someone who has a *predominantly external locus of control* tends to blame the outside world for nearly all things that happen in their life. As with any two polar opposites, you can see that these tendencies can have a negative impact on your life. For example, someone with a high internal locus of control tends to blame and beat themselves up when things don't go their way, even if they have no control over the outcome. It is important to recognize that there are things that we do not have control over.

On the other side of the spectrum, someone with a high external locus of control tends to not take responsibility for anything, blaming everyone else for things that are clearly within their control. They don't take control of their life because they do not think that they have the power to make a difference.

The goal is to have a balanced locus of control so that you have a realistic view of what you have power over. Below is a small list of things that you have control over right now:

How much effort you put into something.	How many times you smile, say thank you, or show appreciation today.	How well you prepare for something.
How you react to an emotion.	What you focus on.	How you interpret a situation.
What you commit to doing or not doing.	What conversations you have and what you engage in.	How much you focus on in the present moment.
What you tell yourself and how nice you are to *you*.	How you take care of your body.	How many new things you are exposed to.
What you do in your free time.	Whom you spend your time with and who your friends are.	What information you consume, the books you read, the media you listen to or watch.
When you ask for help.	How much you believe what other people say.	How long it takes you to try again when you fail.

Now this is just a small list of examples. However, notice that all these items are directly related to *you*. Yes, *you*. Your thoughts, beliefs, emotions, actions, and choices are all within your circle of control. Remember that some of the things that you have control over have consequences, but those consequences do not take away from the fact that you have a choice.

 ### EMPOWERful Questions

What are things that you have control over that you would want to change and take charge of?

_____

_____

_____

_____

How will taking control help you create your new story?

_____

_____

_____

_____

_____

_____

Things You Can Influence

Outside of your circle of control, the next level is your sphere of influence. Our influence and perceived influence are critical to our well-being. In fact, researchers Dr. Sommer and Dr. Bourgeois have been able to show that the more influential you feel you are, the greater your happiness and well-being. This is because feeling that we influence others gives us a sense of purpose, meaning, and control. Notice that *influence* is different from *control*. Influence doesn't mean telling people what to do or making them do something. That does not lead to happiness. And, if we are keeping it 100, you can't make people do anything, not a damn thing!

I do believe in the exchange of energies. When you raise your vibration, you're going to make people who vibrate at a low level uncomfortable. There are two ways that you can increase your level of happiness when it comes to your influence:

1. ***Increase your influence on others around you***. The type of influence we're talking about here is being a leader in our inner circle, meaning leading by example. For example, when we follow our dreams, we stand up for what we believe, and when we grow, we empower others around us to do the same. It is about living in the reality that if you change your behavior or attitude, other people tend to notice and are affected by those changes whether they want to or not.

2. ***Increase your awareness of how you currently influence those around you***. When you acknowledge the positive impact you are having on others, it boosts your confidence.

I was able to influence the culture within the organization I worked for so that children were placed at a higher rate with their relatives and relative placements were advocated for, whereas, previous to my leadership, children were being adopted in high percentages in non-related and transracial homes. This troubled me deeply and I worked hard at shifting the mindset of my staff to embrace, advocate, and support relative placements. When I left Alameda County Social Services, I walked away with a sense of gratitude and accomplishment for the influence I had within my department.

Influence is a normal part of human nature. It's up to you to decide in what ways you are influenced by others and whether you are a good influence on those around you. The sphere of influence goes both ways because the people that you may have influenced also influence you. Choose wisely who you are around and be aware of the impact you have on others.

 ## EMPOWERful Action & Questions

Make a list of those closest to whom you influence and/or who influence you:

1._____

2._____

3._____

4._____

5._____

How do you influence them (both positively and negatively)?

_____

_____

_____

_____

_____

How can you become a better positive influence on them?

_____

_____

_____

_____

_____

How do they influence you (both positively and negatively)?

_____

_____

_____

_____

Are there any negative influences that you can replace with positive ones?

_____

_____

_____

_____

How do you influence people in other areas of your life (work, school, organizations, family, church, etc.)?

_____

_____

_____

_____

Becoming a positive influence will increase your happiness and well-being. Owning your story and owning your power will serve as an empowering example to others. Be mindful of the company you keep and any negative influencers in your life that may hinder the story that you are creating for yourself.

It takes courage to be your authentic self. It takes courage to sometimes stand out from the pack. If you don't wanna shake it up a bit, be mediocre, be normal, and fit in. Talk like them, think what they think, be where they are, go where they go, and be a clone like Tyrone, a copycat. Once you have nullified your uniqueness, you don't need courage. I say, "Don't sacrifice your authenticity for other people's approval!" Always stay true to yourself. You ain't gotta try to prove something or be something else for anybody. For me, I had to learn the hard way.

It takes courage to be different. It takes courage to change things that don't work and serve you any longer. It takes courage to try scary things, but really, it's in the mind. I believe all of us have what it takes, we all have demonstrated that we have courage. Get comfortable with leaning into it. Do the impossible. Do you have the courage to bet on yourself?

Own Your Story - Power With a Plan -Write Your Story

Owning your story is the key to owning your inner power. We all have a story and whether you keep it to yourself or write a book, you have to allow yourself to be heard. We all have something that makes us unique. We all have different paths that we will travel in this life. Each person's story is an accumulation of choices and experiences. Even two people who have had similar lives will have slightly different experiences. We all have a fascinating story to tell.

Writing a memoir to read privately, to share with friends or family, or to publish, is gratifying on so many levels. It helps you gain perspective on your experiences while sharing your authentic unique self. We all have the carnal need to be heard, and writing your story allows you to meet that need. When you finish you may be surprised at what you've accomplished.

Many years ago, when I started on my journey of self-discovery I worked with my first life coach. One of my assignments was to write my life story. I didn't know it then, but that assignment transformed me. It was healing as it included my good, bad, ugly, and everything in between. It helped me see into myself, how I came to where I was at the time. The beauty is that our story continues and hopefully, when we are no longer here on Earth, our legacy will continue. What is your story? What is the legacy you want to leave?

Writing your story will take some time and you have to be intentional. Remember, when you write, have self-compassion for yourself, especially when writing about traumatic events. Writing your story may help your family know you better or they may understand themselves more through reading about your experiences. Regardless of how you use your story, this exercise is expressing yourself in a permanent way, giving yourself a gift for letting your true unique authentic voice be heard.

I wonder at times about *who* I've been in my life journey and all the different roles I've played. I'd like to think I've been positively regarded in all my interactions; however, in reality, there have been plenty of scenarios where I'm a villain. Yes, I do take accountability for my actions, however, at the end of the day how people see me is more about them than me. We often see people through our perspectives that have been shaped by our beliefs and values. It is also impacted by our life experiences in general. Just like two people can look at the same painting and see something different. Some people may see your bright personality as captivating, while others may see it as overbearing and you doing too much. Some people think you're rude and selfish, and others respect the way you set boundaries and take care of yourself.

Lisa Nichols said, "I have nothing to hide, nothing to prove, nothing to defend, and nothing to protect." I love that quote because it keeps it at the forefront that we can't allow others to dictate our actions or our beliefs about ourselves. People are going to have opinions about you. I stopped trying to tend to all the opinions of others or let them affect how I feel about myself; good, bad, or indifferent. I cannot control others' thoughts about me. Actually, what they think about me ain't my business. My focus is me doing and being me and creating all the joy my heart and arms can hold.

When you master the ability to own your story, you own your power! When you own your power, you can achieve all your goals and you get more than just your desired outcome, you also find your inner strength, and my dear, this is the zone of *honoring yourself.* You now have the power to overcome obstacles and live a powerful and mindful life. This requires you to practice who you desire to be. You don't wake up one morning and suddenly you're who you think you want to be. You have to put some energy into it.

I want you to imagine that you have achieved your goal. Imagine you are that successful version of yourself now. ***What can you see, hear, and feel?***

_____

_____

_____

_____

_____

_____

_____

_____

_____

_____

Now, visualize the steps you took to get there, including the point where you are now, making that initial decision. Go back to the future and think about your feelings. Imagine how confident you feel now that you have achieved your goals. Feel how motivated you are and how inspired you are to achieve more. Think about all the positive feelings you have now.

Take these feelings and put them in the first step (the image you created for the first step) and then the second, and third until you find yourself in the image that represents the successful you.

How are you honoring your true authentic self?

_____

_____

_____

_____

_____

_____

_____

Daily journaling facilitates reflection and sparks useful brainstorming about how to better strive toward your goals and release thoughts and emotions you're experiencing. Here's an acronym I've learned that is a great way to remember the ways journaling will be the heavy-lifting tool you can use to level up.

J- Judgment Free

Write what is in your heart. This is private, personal, and a safe place for you to express your thoughts and feelings without judgment.

O-Observation

Journaling is a great opportunity to be the observer of self. As a prompt, you can write what happened to you and how you think about what that means for you.

U-Understanding

Piggyback on observing what happened, how we perceive how something happened is more important to what happened to us. When we are aware of our thoughts and their patterns, we are able to master them.

R-Revelation

This process can lead to revelations about our desires, our dreams, our goals, and our aspirations. It can help us get clear with our true authentic selves.

N-Needs Assessment

Keeping a journal makes it easier to notice problems and potential solutions, as the simple act of writing something down can make it simpler and clearer. Keeping things stuffed inside is harmful on many levels.

A-Awareness

Writing about your experiences helps you take a wider perspective on your life, as well as reminding you of problem areas and things you have to be grateful for. Raising awareness is the first step toward making the transformation you desire.

L-Life

Journaling is known to be an effective way to de-stress. Just a few minutes a day can have a major impact on your health and happiness.

Sis, at the end of the day this is *your* life. You are responsible for your life and if you're sitting around waiting for somebody to save you, to fix you, to even help you, you are wasting your time because only *you* have the power to take responsibility to move your life forward!

Each day I am clear that I'm responsible for myself. I'm responsible for how I feel and I'm responsible for the energy I bring to the world. I know hurt people hurt people, so I have to heal so I won't leak my pain onto other people. I realized that I had the power all along and all I had to do was use it. Lastly, I've learned that I have to define success for myself because everyone has their own perception of what that means and looks like. I'm at a point on my journey where I am making decisions for my happiness that may not make sense to people around me, and *that's okay.*

I am not looking for a high five or words of encouragement. I'm not asking people what they think about it. I'm just gonna do it so if you see me doing something out of character or I'm acting brand new just know it's about who I'm becoming and not about who I've been. It's about where I'm going and not where I was, and I don't want anybody to take it personally when this growth happens.

I'm at a point right now where you're just going to have to accept me. For me, my personality is no longer up for negotiation. I'm not going to keep catering to how other people feel about me or tiptoeing around their perceptions of me. I'm simply going to be showing up as my authentic self, 100% of the time.

Own Your Story Without the Cape

Can we please drop the strong Black woman narrative, please?! You don't have to be strong any longer, ladies. Be soft, be flowers, be dolls, be vulnerable, be taken care of. That strong Black woman thing is a trick that they sell you so that they can load you with stress and then expect you to be able to bounce back from it. You don't bounce back, you go to therapy, you heal, you close yourself off, you recuperate, you embrace your comeback but what you're not going to do is to be strong for somebody else's challenges!

I am the first to say I marched around with my Superwoman, strong Black woman cape proudly. I proudly shared my struggles and all the trials and tribulations I experienced and felt it was an honor to wear the "resilient" badge. It was like Girl Scouts, and I was collecting those badges. But now my perspective has shifted. I don't find it flattering when you call me resilient. I was so exhausted by my strength. I was at the stage of being emotionally and physically worn out.

I know that yes, *strong* is a strength but it can be a curse. If everyone thinks we are so strong then we can't ask for help, nor do we think we deserve it. I do appreciate my resilience to still be here to tell my story and I am appreciative to know that living a life of 'ease' is not only desired but also attainable. I am worthy of ease, peace, joy, love, wellness, and abundance and nothing else is even an option. So don't call me *strong*.

Now it's me embracing that I am somebody's fine-ass auntie. I'm 52 and I tell myself, "Stop trying to get back to the old you. She doesn't exist anymore; she has left the building. What you've been through, what you've experienced, has changed you. You're different now. You're wiser. You're much smarter. You understand people differently now. You see people and read energy now. Your worldview has changed. It's broader, it's inclusive. You're also not into the same things anymore. (#mute R. Kelly)." Different things excite me now, like expanding my creativity and connecting with my spirituality. Being unapologetic about everything I do is now so freeing. My third eye is open and I'm loving the 50's Club.

My ex-husband would say to me in frustration, "You've changed!" Yep, buddy, I did. I have. I am not the same person anymore. I am a whole new me. I have embraced her. She is pretty dope and I love her. Look at the person in the mirror. Embrace that person and own your brilliance. Remember you are the story creator. By combining the wisdom of forgiveness, the recognition of teachable moments, and a thoughtful approach to personal agency, it's your time to take action to proactively own your story and powers.

EMPOWER

CHAPTER 6

Well-Being - Caring for Yourself

Well-being, like everything else, starts with your mindset. To care for ourselves and achieve the balance we require and desire, we must cultivate the practice of tending to our well-being. Our well-being is directly connected to our health. Health is the *real* wealth if you are a paper chaser. If you are not well physically, mentally, emotionally, and spiritually, well, it doesn't take a rocket scientist to know that nothing else matters without your well-being.

I am a fan of Abraham Hicks. She is the Law of Attraction guru and one of her famous quotes is, "So when people say, "What are you doing? You say, "Things that please me." And they say, "Toward what end?" And you say, "Pleasure." And they say, "But really, what are you working on?" And you say, "Having a good time." And they say, "But what do you hope to accomplish?" And you say, "Living happily ever after."

That's me. I've made the conscious decision to live happily ever after, and most importantly, happily in the moment. Well-being is subjective, so how I prefer to tend to my well-being may be very different from what you do. Certainly, there can be an argument that there are limitless things people can do to support their well-being. This list is not exhaustive; however, I have found for myself and the women I've coached and counseled that these have been the key to our well-being which equates to being relaxed, recharged, and renewed. Before I take you to these keys, let's spend some time exploring these thinking patterns and behaviors. Do any of these sound familiar?

- You feel like a failure because you aren't doing everything perfectly at home and work.

- You stay awake all night thinking about everything you need to do the next day, week, month, or year.

- Your to-do list is longer than your arm and it never gets shorter.

- You worry that your kids/partner/parent aren't getting enough of your time.

- You stay up late cleaning/cooking/packing lunches/ironing because you can't stand the thought of not getting everything done.

- You find it difficult to say no.

- You shy away from asking for help.

- You find it difficult to take time for yourself.

Sis, you're not alone. In a 2015 study examining stress and coping mechanisms among women of color, 50% of respondents reported feeling high levels of stress. A study published in October 2019 found that 77% of the women respondents reported prioritizing their family's needs over their own, and 48% reported that their burnout was so severe it kept them up at night. If you're a woman, especially a Black woman, then most likely you relish in the role of Superwoman, aka Strong Black Woman.

Cheryl L. Woods-Giscombe wanted to explore the intersections of race and gender. In 2010, she developed a framework she refers to as the Superwoman Schema.

- the obligation to manifest strength.

- the obligation to suppress emotions.

- a resistance to being vulnerable or dependent

- a determination to succeed despite limited resources.

- feeling an obligation to help others.

She says, "Being able to be the rock and the strength of the family, 'the glue of the family', is aspirational, and it's often viewed positively among young Black girls and young Black women."

Other perceived benefits:

- Feelings of strength and intelligence.

- It is gratifying that others praise all the things that she can do.

- It feels pleasant to be able to help others.

- Improved self-confidence and motivation.

So I get it. There is a level of satisfaction that we experience when we are in this role. I have come full circle in protecting my well-being. I knew exercising and getting enough sleep were important, but I ignored the other elements that impacted my well-being. For one, my Superwoman cape dictated my ability to experience optimum well-being. I stayed so wound up and busy running from task to task, giving endlessly of myself, because, hey, that's who I am. Despite having a feeling of gratification and at times fulfilling my purpose, I felt overwhelmed and depleted most days.

Unbeknownst to me, I was the typical "Superwoman", a term first coined in 1984. Superwoman Syndrome occurs when a woman neglects herself because she is seeking to "do it all" to perfection and stretches herself too thin. The typical superwomen are moms, professionals, entrepreneurs, wives/partners, caregivers, family members, volunteers, community organizers, and athletes. Let's be frank here: being a *superwoman* is not just unique to Black women, as women in general are feeling this pressure.

It wasn't until I identified what decreased my energy levels that I finally got into alignment. My life now consists of protecting my peace at all costs. Nobody…nobody… (in my Keith Sweat voice) will be able to interfere with it, because I'm not letting them. That includes people, places and things. If it doesn't feel like ease, love, kindness, joy, abundance, or peace, then it, you, them, whoever is blocked, deleted, removed, and ignored.

Again, as we learned earlier in Chapter 2, our body is absorbing all the stress we're experiencing.

It's important to pay attention to what's going on in your body. I often encourage my clients in my practice to pause and get connected to what they are feeling in their bodies. Our bodies are speaking to us. Are you listening? Accumulated stress manifests in a multitude of health issues, including early aging, heart disease, diabetes, obesity, and gastrointestinal conditions.

Time to take off the cape.

- Ask for help.

You're not a machine. You cannot do everything yourself.

It's not weak to ask for help.

- Take time out for you.

Schedule breaks into your calendar and hold yourself to it. Daily meditation, mindfulness practice, or yoga will relieve stress and help you to slow down.

- Forget your impulses to control everything.

As much as you try, things will not always work out as you wish. You must leave a space for uncertainty and for things to happen on their own.

- Learn to say *no*.

"No" is not a dirty word. Start saying *no* to things that you don't want, or don't have the time to do. Figure out what your priorities are and say *no* to everything else.

- Remember that everyone is responsible for their own life.

Wanting to help others is fine, but it becomes harmful when you do everything for them.

- Learn to delegate.

Others can also perform tasks and they can perform them well. Do not act as if other people are incompetent. This will only limit their potential to grow.

- Set goals according to how you want to live.

Does it match up with how you want to live your life? If not, list small actions you can take to shift the circle, so it aligns more with your ideals.

Superwoman is a fictional character, not a role model, and trying to be her isn't sustainable or healthy. The protection of your time, space, and peace is your responsibility. You can't get it back when you give it away. Our time is a resource and more valuable than money. Can you think about the last time you gave your time or energy away to someone or something and it left you feeling like crap? Did you feel like a shell of yourself? Can you think of a time you helped someone or contributed to a cause, and you felt empowered, and it boosted your self-confidence, self-esteem, and life satisfaction? The key is to pay attention to how you're feeling before, during and afterward. Let's dig a little deeper.

1. Identify the key to your well-being and achieving balance.

The wheel of life tool helps my clients assess the different areas in their lives. Wellness encompasses theses eight mutually interdependent dimensions:

❖ Physical	❖ Intellectual
❖ Emotional	❖ Social
❖ Spiritual	❖ Vocational
❖ Environmental	❖ Financial

In the first chapter, you looked at where you were in each one of these categories. In this section, we'll look at the four simple evidence-based actions which can improve well-being in everyday life.

1. Give - Your Time, Your Words, Your Presence. When we give service to others, it feeds our soul and spirit. When we stand for others and have an impact on our family, community, or world we are empowered. Now I know you're saying, "Well, you just said don't give your time away and take off the cape." Yes, and yes, and be intentional and mindful. Giving is a gift, just give from the overflow, what has spilled onto the saucer. Leave what's in the cup for you.

2. Be Active. Do what you can. Enjoy what you do. Move your mood. I know you know being active and doing some type of exercise or movement is necessary for your well-being. You might already have your workout system incorporated into your life. If you do, I know you can attest to the many benefits you experience from working out. Don't get caught up in thinking going to the gym is the only form of getting active in your life. I hear so many women say, "I don't like the gym. I feel out of place or intimidated at the gym." That's a mindset block because it's actually pretty amazing all the many forms of physical activities you could do without a gym. There's dancing, walking, hiking, skating, swimming, sports, yoga, pilates, etc. Working out is my happy place. When I don't work out, I can definitely feel the shift in my mood. I've also found that I enjoy all types of physical activity. I've even started taking pole dancing classes. Now, baby, *that's* a workout. The level of upper body and core strength you need to pull yourself up a pole and twirl is massive. P-Valley got me thinking I can fly. Sadly, I cannot, but I'm working at it. I have mad respect for erotic pole dancing because it takes a whole lot of athleticism and skill to do what they do and make it look good.

Here are some key benefits to staying active:

✓ It can help with weight loss

✓ It is good for your muscles and bones

✓ It can increase your energy levels

✓ It can reduce your risk of chronic disease

✓ It can help skin health

✓ It can help your brain health and memory

✓ It can help with relaxation and sleep quality

✓ It can reduce pain

✓ It can promote a better sex life

✓ It can improve your confidence

3. **Keep Learning.** Embrace new experiences. Seek opportunities. Continuous learning is important because it helps people to feel happier and more fulfilled in their lives and careers and to maintain stronger cognitive functioning when they get older. Whenever you learn something new, the neurons in your brain actually make new connections. This is called neuroplasticity. Once this happens, your brain will easily adjust to new situations or any change in your environment. I once worked with a client who felt like she was too old to go back to school to finish her degree. We talked about her fears and concerns, and she recognized that living a life of regret was indeed unfulfilling. There was a longing within her to finish her education as a registered nurse. She went on to complete nursing school and is doing what she had longed to do. She's excited about all the new things she's learning at the hospital and eager to learn other aspects of the profession, in addition to her income increasing exponentially.

4. **Take Notice.** Appreciate the little things. Savor the moment. Living in the moment and living in the now is all we really have. Cultivating the attitude of gratitude is making a conscious habit of expressing appreciation for big and small things regularly. When we are taking notice, we are not worried about the future, tripping on the past, or anxious about the future. We are tapping into the appreciation of the present moment. I've shared earlier that exercise 54321 is my favorite mindfulness activity to do. It's an opportunity for me to appreciate the five senses we are gifted with and, most importantly, I get to experience the appreciation of what I'm focusing on. It's an endless gift of possibilities of appreciation.

It's important to note that these components are interconnected and influence each other. Achieving well-being requires attention and balance in all these areas, and the relative importance of each component may vary from person to person. Additionally, well-being is a dynamic process that evolves, and individuals may experience different challenges and priorities at different stages of their lives.

We have to work hard at our well-being and in fact, it's not our natural default to be in this state. We can get fleeting moments at times when we feel the boat is steady, but for the majority of us, life is tricky and bumpy. As a result, our emotions are challenged in the regulation department. As we learned earlier, we are creatures of habit and life has a way of keeping us on autopilot, so to achieve this oh-so-elusive balance, you have to be intentional. It requires daily practice, and it requires your commitment to yourself. Have you ever heard the saying that you need five hobbies? One to make you money, one to keep you in shape, one to keep you creative, one to build your knowledge, and one to evolve your mindset!

Ask yourself, how am I currently tending to my well-being? What will it take?

_____

_____

_____

_____

_____

Identification of Areas for Improvement

Here you will identify your energy zappers. In Chapter 2, you started some of this by listing what you love and loathe. Now is the time to commit to really getting rid of or significantly reducing the energy zappers in your life.

List three habits or tasks that zap your energy:

1._____

2._____

3._____

How will eliminating or changing these habits impact or improve your life?

_____

_____

_____

_____

_____

_____

Making changes to better support your well-being is necessary. Sorry, not sorry, if this feels redundant, but again, making changes is necessary for your well-being. You don't have to freak out and have the worry of, "Will I stay consistent?" The short answer to that worry is you will likely fall off and that is *perfectly fine*. We are shooting for progress, not perfection. Small changes make a big impact. Daily action and commitment are necessary. Soon these small changes will be part of your lifestyle and your authentic self.

In the exercise below you will come up with three new success habits. For the sake of this exercise, select a habit that supports your well-being.

1._____

2._____

3._____

How are you making time for these?

_____

_____

_____

_____

Learn How to Create Healthy/Helpful Habits and Eliminate the Others

Our habits are our systems of everyday flow. Healthy habits are those repetitive actions or behaviors you want to repeat. They have positive physical, emotional, or psychological consequences. Oftentimes we are held back with habits that do not help us. They actually have the opposite effect. Some habits we have keep us stuck and keep us from accomplishing our goals. They also put your health, both physical and psychological, at risk and are the ultimate energy zappers. Have you ever thought about a habit you had like snacking when stressed, binge-watching Netflix when you have a project to complete, or waiting until the last minute to do something that you've been avoiding? If you answered yes, you're not alone. I believe most people have dealt with these types of pesky habits; I certainly have. I really had procrastination bad, I mean *bad* bad. I feel like I adopted the habit during college and because the results turned out good in most cases, it reinforced the habit. Many moons ago during my undergraduate studies, I would wait until the last minute to start writing my papers. I would do my research and gather all my sources, but I wouldn't start the paper until the night before it was due. This approach was very stressful, but I convinced myself I did better work under pressure. I liked the monkey on my back. I would pull all-nighters all the time. I even walked a paper in while wearing my pajamas. This approach continued during my graduate studies, but my results did not pan out as well as they did in my undergraduate studies. My results appeared rushed and sloppy, and I realized that waiting until the last minute was not producing my best work and the stress, insomnia, and poor eating habits exacerbated my poor mood. Slowly I started a different approach, paced myself, worked in batches, and stuck to my study schedule. When I did that, my performance improved, and I felt good about myself and my results. Also, I became more aware of myself and because it didn't just look like procrastination it showed up in other ways. I later learned I have adult attention deficit disorder. I'm able to have grace when I'm feeling really stretched to stay focused and I remind myself I like the results when I'm intentionally choosing to get in action instead of delaying.

Don't get me wrong, procrastination still surfaces from time to time, and we'll get more into how to eliminate or minimize your tendency to procrastinate later in this chapter. This is an example of a habit that manifested from a disorder that wasn't helpful, but some habits do help us. For example, working out in the morning before I do anything else is a habit that has improved my life tremendously. I used to believe I wasn't a morning person. I did my best work at night and considered myself a night owl. Going to bed super late prevented me from getting up in the morning and I would feel groggy. It was all in my mind because when I trained for my bodybuilding competition, I worked out at 5:30 AM every morning and I loved how I felt for the rest of the day. The other connection was my *why*. I had a reason 'why' I was getting up. I had a goal in mind, a target. You've got to get clarity on your 'why'.

In reflection, can you identify some areas in your life to improve or increase or to remove or decrease? Now it's about making it a permanent part of your life. To assist in learning the science of habits and how to really make a habit stick, read *Atomic Habits* by James Clear. I love his point of view that habits are as good as the systems we put in place.

Habit stacking is a concept James discusses, which is putting a habit you want to start doing in between habits you already have. What habit can you put in between or in front of or even after a habit you already have?

Understand we all have the natural resistance to change and I'm going to show you how to overcome that resistance. We are creatures of habit. I'm sure you have heard that saying before. Well, it's very true. Once we have a habit, a way of being, our brains prefer that. For the most part, our brains crave familiarity and certainty. Yet in life to grow and evolve we must identify patterns, beliefs, and behaviors that no longer serve us and do away with them. When it comes to your well-being, being intentional about sticking to helpful habits and kicking the unhelpful ones is essential to your best life. Another way to look at our habits is in the framework of the 3 R's of Habit Loops that James Clear references in *Atomic Habit:*

1. **The Reminder**: All our habits have triggers, and these triggers initiate the behavior.

2. **The Routine**: This is the actual habit, action, or routine that you have.

3. **The Reward**: This is the benefit that you get from the actual behavior. Keep in mind that negative consequences have benefits and serve as a reward.

Refer to the Wheel of Life action you committed to doing. Let's look at the health section and make those actions a habit. List your top action and answer the questions for each "action/habit."

Step 1: Set a reminder for your new habit.

Will you set a reminder using an alarm or notification? If not, what are some simple healthy habits that you already have that you do every day? How can you integrate your new habit into one of them?

_____

_____

_____

_____

_____

Step 2: Make it a routine.

If your new habit is something you need to schedule in, where and how are you going to set aside time for it? What else do you need to prepare in advance so that you have everything you need at the scheduled time to get up and go? How can you protect this new routine?

_____

_____

_____

_____

_____

_____

Step 3: Create a reward.

Does your habit have a built-in reward? If so, what? What are some ideas of things you could reward yourself for meeting certain milestones? For instance, every time you make it a week performing a new habit, you give yourself something special, whether it's something you do that you enjoy or a small gift to yourself.

_____

_____

_____

_____

_____

Recently, a client shared that instead of rewarding herself with an activity or small gift, she rewarded herself with words of affirmation. Shifting her self-talk and sense of self-worth has been the focus of our work together. This is the personal work that's most important to her.

What are three important milestones or sub-goals you will reach on your way to your well-being habit?

1._____

2._____

3._____

What are three ideas you could do to celebrate/reward your accomplishments?

1._____

2._____

3._____

Play Time: What are three activities you can add to your schedule every week to plan in fun and balance?

1._____

2._____

3._____

Putting Money Aside: In what ways could you put money aside to use to reward yourself?

_____

_____

_____

_____

_____

_____

_____

_____

Unplug: In what ways can you plan time free of electronics? What are some plug-free activities you would like to do more of?

_____

_____

_____

_____

_____

4. Change is Necessary

We are in the middle of the book, so if you're feeling a little dip and a resistance to change or move forward, you're in good company. During the process when we are establishing new behaviors and habits, there will be some tendency to resist, to "relapse" or fall all the way off. I know I've been guilty of this many times in my life as it relates to eating healthily, especially letting go of sweets, even more specifically chocolate. I will do well for a while, then boom I see it and I go in, and I'm back on the eating chocolate cycle, until I say, "Hey! Enough is enough, cut it off."

When we stop old habits, they can creep back on us because we miss them like old friends. For example, most addictions begin by way of the need to avoid an intense and uncomfortable feeling, so it makes stopping, at least initially, uncomfortable. We as humans don't like discomfort. This is because humans are hardwired to resist change and seek pleasure. Our brain perceives change as a threat. Because of this, it activates our system's fight or flight response. Even in the long run, stopping an unhelpful habit and replacing it with a different habit will be beneficial to us. And yet we are resistant. Letting go of habits is also in the same boat as letting go of people who are not healthy for our well-being. For example, for many years my resistance to leave my last marriage kept me in an insidious loop of frustration and pain, yet I was not able to walk away. It takes work, it takes inner strength but most of all, it takes an inner belief that you are worthy, you are worth it, and you deserve kindness, wellness, and peace.

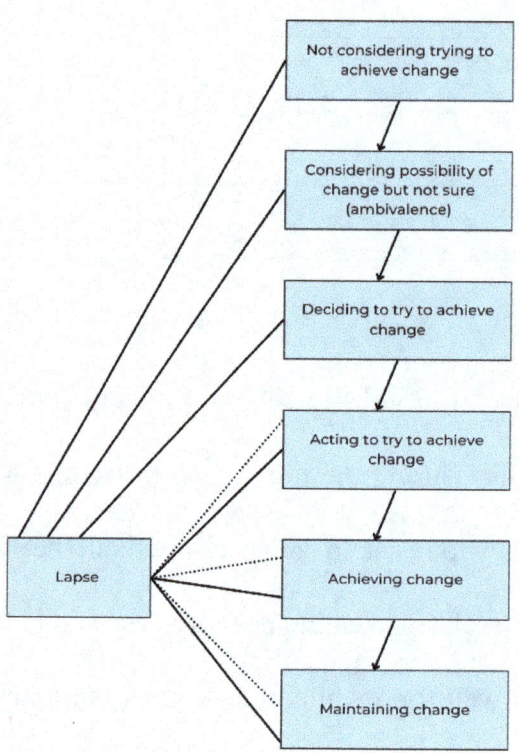

To give you a visual of the normal process of change, this flowchart is an original creation of David Bonham-Carter and can be found in his eBook *Changing Your Life: A Practical Guide*. It is based on the ideas and research of James Prochaska and Carlo DiClemente.

What I want you to get from this is that it's OK- it's going to happen, and you *still can/will* adapt to new habits/thoughts/feelings/behaviors with intentionality and practice.

5. *Procastor the Troll* Has to Go!

Procastor the Troll is the dude who lives under the bridge and keeps you from doing what you desire to do. Every time you're about to get it done, he jumps out and stops you from crossing and handling your business. *Procastor the Troll* is your inner critic's first cousin. You've been successful in getting rid of her, the inner critic, time to do the same for her cousin, the troll.

Having unhealthy habits does not help your well-being and procrastinating can certainly have a negative impact on your well-being. We all have put off doing something we were tasked to do in our lives, right? Most times when we do this, we start the self-defeating thoughts, the guilt, the panic; it can be a vicious cycle. And although it may seem senseless to put ourselves in these predicaments, we usually see some form of short-term benefit, some type of pleasure. Everything we do in life is linked to the 'pain/pleasure principle' and I'm not talking about the hit by Janet Jackson (although that's my jam and I'm dating myself).

If you are continuing a pattern or habit you don't like, it's because you are linking more pain to stopping it than you are to continuing it. If in the *moment* isn't causing you enough pain to stop doing it, (procrastinating) then you need to link it in your mind to the pain - failure, embarrassment, disappointment, or heartache - that you'll feel if you keep doing it.

The bottom line is if you don't take action because of the pain you associate with it, start focusing on the pain you will experience by not taking action and associate pleasure with the outcome you desire, which in this case is *doing* whatever it is that you have been procrastinating about.

Since procrastination is one of the top problems my clients battle with, I created a program called *Uncover Your Procrastination Style and Eradicate It*. Again, everything starts with awareness, and identifying how procrastination is playing out in your life is key before you can dismantle it. As the title suggests, there are styles to your procrastination. Are you a Perfectionist Procrastinator,

Dreamer Procrastinator, Worrier Procrastinator, Defier Procrastinator, Crisis-Maker Procrastinator, or an Over doer Procrastinator? Each style shows up differently and you may even have been all of them at some point in your life. I know that I most definitely have.

My college days were the worst, but I continued to allow procrastination to interfere with my life both personally and professionally. My suffering was not in vain. Luckily, I discovered there are four elements to overcoming procrastination, and to help with recognizing them, they all start with an R.

1. **Retrospection.** Self-awareness on how, when, where, and why.

2. **Rewire.** Uncover and dismantle negative beliefs, shift your mindset.

3. **Realign.** Clarity of purpose, actions aligned with your priorities.

4. **Reward**. Celebrate, enjoy, review, readjust, rinse, and repeat.

I go into more detail about all of this in my course, but you will get the benefit of some of the exercises and prompts to work your way through this issue.

The following are two exercises. The first is called the Procrastination Table to look at how you put off doing things in general. In this exercise, you will identify the actions that you are putting off. I need you to be real with yourself, think about the short-term benefits of each action, and consider other possible things you can say to yourself in this scenario to assist you in following through on the action despite the short-term benefit from doing so. For example, if you are putting off talking to someone about difficulties in the relationship because of the short-term benefit of avoiding immediate confrontation, you might remind yourself that if you don't do so then you are likely to have lots of unvoiced negative feelings towards each other which may lead to even more arguments or an awkward silence.

What is the action you are putting off?	Describe the situation when you are tempted to put off the action.	What are the benefits of putting off the actions?	What can you say to yourself in this situation to help you complete the action? (list possibilities)
1.			
2.			
3.			

Once you have completed the list of what you can say to yourself, pick the statements that are most likely to help and use them when the situation or a similar situation arises again.

The next exercise is to really assist you in getting clear about how you have been showing up for *yourself*. Yes, I said it, *for yourself*. When we don't do the things we know deep down inside that we want to do, we cause our own suffering on multiple levels.

Below is an activity that will help you stop patterns/behaviors/procrastination because you associate massive pain with continuing the old pattern, and you associate massive pleasure with the desirable habit.

What are you currently procrastinating?

_____

_____

_____

_____

Why do you believe you are procrastinating on this?

_____

_____

_____

_____

INSIDE SCOOP- You are avoiding doing it because you associate the task with **pain.**

List one to two patterns or behaviors that you want to change in order to reach your goals/dreams and the desired new behaviors or outcomes:

Unwanted pattern/behavior:

_____

_____

_____

_____

_____

Desired behavior/outcome:

_____

_____

_____

_____

_____

Unwanted pattern/behavior:

_____

_____

_____

_____

Desired behavior/outcome:

_____

_____

_____

_____

Now for each desired change, answer the following questions:

PATTERN 1:

What is the pain you are avoiding by not doing it? (this can be a pain from the experience of making the change and/or the pain you would experience if you did reach your goal.)

_____

_____

_____

_____

_____

_____

What is the pain you experience (or will) with old patterns/behavior/procrastination?

_____

_____

_____

_____

_____

What is the pleasure you've gotten from the pattern or behavior? (what benefits do you receive from keeping this old pattern?)

_____

_____

_____

_____

If you <u>do not</u> stop the pattern or behavior how will it impact your life, your career, your family?

_____

_____

_____

_____

What is the pleasure you will experience if you <u>do</u> stop the pattern and create the desired outcome? (How will your life be better? How will you feel? What weight will be lifted? What other important outcomes will come from this?)

_____

_____

_____

_____

_____

Bottom line: you must get clear on your "why" as this will give you the oomph you need to push through. Perhaps you are avoiding it because it's really not what *you* want. It may be someone else's voice you hear. For years I put this book off because I wanted it to be perfect and then there were parts about me and my story I was ashamed to expose. In addition, I had been advised on different approaches to writing the book. I finally had to get quiet with myself and figure out what my issue was with finishing this book, what the purpose of the book was, why was it important for me to write this book, and what I really wanted to share. Once I did that, it was like I was instantly inspired and excited to write this book again.

It's a matter of shifting your thoughts about it. Short-term thinking says the donut tastes good. Eat it. Short-term thinking says one workout doesn't matter. I can skip it. Short-term thinking encourages you to make short-term emotional decisions that hurt you in the long run. Yet, thinking strategically is key. Think long-term. Act strategically. Take action that improves your long-term position and moves you toward your long-term goals.

I try to refrain from using the term "need" to describe a desired action because it has a tone of judgment. However, I just could not find a different way to say these next recommendations. So if it sounds a bit judgy, know it comes from a place of care and love. You need to love yourself unconditionally. You need to choose yourself, *unapologetically*. You need to move your body. You need to heal and fill your soul. You need to read, study, and practice. You need to know your strategic goals and you need to know why they are important to you. You need to get up, get out of your damn head, get off your phone, get out of the soft and addictive comfort zone, and go out there into the world and get after it. Quit playing games with yourself. This is your life!

Do *You*, Commit to *You*

I call this the *Do You, Boo* section. This is about you accepting that your well-being, your inner wellness, starts with your ability to "Do You" and "Put the oxygen mask on first". You'll lose yourself trying to please other people. You'll lose other people when you choose yourself and if they have to become casualties of the war for your peace then so be it. Our Superwoman cape is killing us, and it has killed our loved ones. Stop now, love yourself, take care of yourself. It starts with doing at least one desired leisure activity once a week. Truthfully, *daily*. Like, what are we doing, people? You *have* to schedule joy in your life and make it a non-negotiable.

Well-being is intentional. Look back at Chapter 3 where you listed what you love and loathe and your 'What Makes Your Heart Sing' list from Chapter 4. Time to make what you love real. Do what you love and love what you do. If one of your wishes is to create a balanced lifestyle, then you must do some things every day and week to meet your own needs. You choose, you decide. It could be relaxing, activating, exercising, or something mentally stimulating or something to help you unwind. Remember, make it fun and do whatever feels good. Do you, Boo Boo.

In the new phase of my life, I am only interested in doing things that bring me pleasure and joy. I know I deserve to live life and enjoy it to the fullest. Recently I've gotten back into roller skating and it's so much fun. I'm not able to do any tricks but I can groove and glide a little without falling. Not only do I enjoy it, I enjoy seeing others skate. I enjoy people-watching. It's a little nostalgic because when I was a young adult that's what we did. Oakland to the Manteca Skating Rink was a regular pastime. The guys were the most fly to see, zooming around the rink so effortlessly, grooving, in sync.

Another funny story about me "doing me" and taking my well-being and happiness into my own hands: Many years ago, my ex-husband and I were vacationing in Costa Rica for the first time. It wasn't unusual for us to have at least one big falling out on our vacations. If you haven't picked up on it yet, I like adventure, and I enjoy being active and the outdoors. Island nature is my happy place. I had always wanted to go ziplining and saw at our resort they offered a tour of the zipline jungle. Once I saw the brochure, like a kid at Disneyland, I shared the information with my ex. He was not impressed and not a fan of the idea. He wasn't interested in doing that activity so he wasn't going, and the other group that was supposed to be on the bus with me canceled so I would have been on that particular bus by myself, and he felt it was a safety issue. I saw his concern and felt it was really unwarranted. A bit of a back and forth between us ensued as I tried to explain why it was a good idea for me to go, because, hell, I wanted to go, and I felt like it was a once-in-a-lifetime opportunity. The disagreement escalated into us talking loudly in a gift shop, then the argument spilled outside to the parking lot, then he doubled down by yelling at me and scolding me, saying that I don't listen, I'm "disobedient and disruptive" and that he made a mistake in marrying me because I don't do what he tells me to do as a wife should. I doubled down as well and told him he could not tell me what to do, I was grown, and I was going zip-lining. And I did. I had an absolutely fantastic time.

When I got to the ziplining park, the place looked like Disneyland in the jungle. There was a convenience store, a gift shop, and even a photo store for you to get a DVD of your ziplining adventure because of course they record it for you and have it ready for you at the end, just like at the big amusement parks. It felt exhilarating to fly through the air; I even hung upside down during one of the least difficult zips. When I got back from the tour, he was still very salty with me for the rest of the trip, ignoring me, and giving me the silent treatment. Despite the discomfort for the rest of the trip, I was still happy with my decision to choose my own happiness, which in essence is a measure of my overall well-being.

Current Leisure Activities

Getting to the fun can be fun. I once worked with a client who wanted to focus on creating more fun in her life. To her it felt like, everything was centered around work. I suggested she create a list of all the things that intrigued her. She took it a step further and created herself a "Playlist Jar." She made different categories of fun such as a new city to visit, cooking a new dish, pampering herself, and something that involved fitness, nature, etc. She wrote down several ideas, cut them up using different colors, folded them, and put them in a jar. Each week she pulled one out and proceeded with the fun.

List in the table below activities that you currently do in your spare time. Who else do you do them with? Roughly how often/for how long do you do them?

Leisure Activity	Who I Do the Activity With	Usual Frequency of the Activity

Possible Other Activities

List any other activities that you might like to do. These might be things you have done before but stopped for one reason or another or it might be something you have never tried before but might like to do.

Leisure Activity	Who I Do the Activity With	Usual Frequency of the Activity

Deciding What to Do

After looking at the above tables, make a list of those leisure activities you are going to try out or explore over the next couple of weeks:

Leisure Activity	When will I do it in the next couple of weeks?	What action will I take to make this a possibility?

What desired leisure activity will you do once a week/daily?

_____

_____

_____

_____

If you could add one more to your weekly/daily list, which activity would it be?

_____

_____

_____

What action could you take to make that happen?

_____

_____

_____

What activity or activities will you do to be active?

_____

_____

_____

_____

_____

What activity or activities will you do to give your time, service, etc.?

_____

_____

_____

_____

_____

What activity or activities will you do to keep learning?

_____

_____

_____

_____

_____

What activity or activities will you do to take notice?

_____

_____

_____

_____

_____

What activity or activities will you do every day?

_____

_____

_____

_____

_____

What activity or activities will you do every month?

_____

_____

_____

_____

How will you create the space and time to do this activity daily, weekly, and monthly?

_____

_____

_____

_____

What do you need to put in place to ensure you stick with this commitment?

_____

_____

_____

_____

_____

Imagine success and take small intentional steps.

- Instead of doing fifty pushups per day, start with five.

- Instead of switching to a new diet, add a vegetable to every lunch.

- Instead of running on a treadmill for thirty minutes per day, start with walking for 5-10 minutes.

Always focus on establishing the actual habit behavior first. Never increase your effort before it has become a natural part of what you do every day.

Remember to:

- ✓ Celebrate your small wins.

- ✓ Have clear intentions.

- ✓ Get hooked on your habit.

- ✓ Start ridiculously small.

- ✓ Design your environment.

Other tips:

Decrease the activation energy of your desired habit (i.e. reading books). For example, put a great book next to your bedroom nightstand or have your Audible queued up for your commute.

Increase the activation energy of your undesired habit of social media. For example, putting the control settings to alert and reduce your usage. Give yourself specific days and times to review. Allow yourself a detox and total abstinence for time limits. By changing the activation energy of your behaviors, you can nudge yourself in the right direction.

- Use "habit stacking." Link your new habit to an already existing behavior by filling in this sentence: "After/Before [established habit] _____, I will [new habits]_____." For example, "After I leave the office, I will go for a brisk walk."

- Implement scheduling. This one might seem obvious, but very few people actually use it. What gets scheduled, gets done. So if your habit is truly important to you, let your calendar reflect that. Give it space in your schedule, just like you would with an important business meeting.

Surround Yourself with Supporters. Research has shown that we tend to feel the same way, and adopt the same goals, as the people we spend the most time with. So, one way to dramatically increase your chances of success is to make sure you have the right people in your corner. Use your Thrive Tribe, accountability partners, EMPOWERED BY COURAGE – Boss Ladies Seeking Limitless Possibilities FB community, friends, family, and yours truly as your resources.

Other Strategies to Help You Pre-Commit to Your Habit

We don't like to lose resources like money, at least I know I don't. As a little motivation to help your workout commitment, send a friend $25 every time you fail to get to the gym before work. Or, to stick to your workout plan for thirty days, declare publicly to your family/blog readers/Facebook friends. Remember self-care is not selfish!

Are you taking the time to make sure you are #1 on your list? Put the oxygen mask on first. And choose you …. unapologetically. Here are more ideas for you to do *you*!

Go for a walk	Take a drive out of state
Buy yourself something special	Read a book (Audible works too)
Take a bubble bath	Light some candles and listen to music to clear your mind, close your eyes, and take a deep breath.
Exercise	Relax in your favorite chair
Sit in front of the fireplace with a cup of tea, coffee, or hot chocolate.	Do some gardening or tend to your houseplants.

Play with your pet(s).	Play with your child(ren), niece(s), or nephew(s).
Go see a movie.	Take a nap.
Sit in a park or a calm area that takes you close to nature.	Cuddle up to your best friend (BFF, partner, pet, etc.) and just quietly enjoy each other.
Realize that being alone is good for you.	Go to a museum or art exhibit.
Get a message/foot reflexology.	Try a new hobby/craft.

Add more:

1.

2.

3.

4.

5.

6.

7.

8.

9.

10.

Time to schedule them in your calendar - day and time! Sis, focus on your commitment to yourself, focus on being determined to commit to yourself.

I took a class at the pole dancing studio. Typically, I only take the Intro to Pole class, but I wanted to explore something different. Little did I know this class was advanced. The instructor had a very strong accent that sounded like she was from Russia or Germany. As she started the warmup it seemed that she had a background in ballet because of the type of stretching and warm-up exercises we were doing. As the class progressed, the instructor and the other women in the class were moving and twirling through the routines. Me, well, I was trying the best I could, and I just could not catch on. Talk about frustration! They'll hit the move and would be on the floor and I'd still be standing like what happened? I've always prided myself on being able to dance, having rhythm, and being a quick learner, but this class challenged me like never before. At the end of each class, I was thankful it was over. I survived. Each class I felt like I wanted to quit, I felt bratty and flat-out pissed, but I kept coming back.

In one particular class, my frustration level rose to the max and I thought, "I can't do this shit and I'm out of here." I walked to the side of the class, sat down, and proceeded to take off my red 7-inch patent leather stiletto boots. I unlaced my left one and took it off and started on the right. Then my inner voice said, "What are you doing? You're not a fucking quitter! You don't quit because it's hard! You don't quit because you're uncomfortable! Put these damn shoes back on and get your ass back into the game!" So, I did and finished the class. I still looked pitiful, but I finished. Afterward, a few of the ladies from the class came to me, shared their support of me, and encouraged me to continue. That's when I learned I was in an advanced class and that many stayed away from the class because of the level of difficulty. I also learned that the women in the class all had one to five years of experience whereas I only had five weeks. The bottom line is that the classes were fun but challenging and that's my focus, fun. I'm here for the fun times.

Well-being is about protecting your peace. People need to be introduced to the new version of you that protects that part. I'm like Jay Z...*Let me reintroduce myself.* I don't have time to be in low vibrational conversations, gossiping, pettiness, and playing the victim. I have a low tolerance for excuses. This version of me really doesn't care about what other people think, because peace is her priority. If it doesn't feel like love or joy, peace or kindness, keep it away from me. It ain't for me. Aht, aht, get somebody else to do it.

Well-being is having the awareness that what you focus on grows and what you focus on, expands. If you focus on the goodness in your life, you create more of it and if you live with an open palm rather than a closed fist, you leave room for immeasurable blessings to flow through your hands.

EMPOWER

CHAPTER 7

Excited And Explore - Accepting and Accelerating Yourself

Welcome to this chapter, where we embark on a journey of self-discovery and personal growth. In the following pages, we will delve into various topics that will ignite your excitement and inspire you to explore new horizons.

We begin by diving deep into the core of your being—your beliefs, values, and purpose. By examining these fundamental aspects, you will gain clarity and insight into what truly drives and motivates you. Understanding your personal beliefs and values will enable you to align your actions with your authentic self, leading to a more fulfilling and purpose-driven life.

Next, we encourage you to create a playlist—a collection of dreams, goals, and experiences that you aspire to achieve. This list will serve as a roadmap for your personal growth and provide you with a sense of direction and inspiration. By documenting your aspirations, you will be more likely to turn them into reality and live a life filled with meaningful experiences.

Just like a captivating movie, your life has a unique storyline. We encourage you to reflect on the narrative of your life, celebrate your triumphs, learn from your challenges, and embrace the adventures that lie ahead. By viewing your life as a movie, you can gain a fresh perspective and approach each day with a renewed sense of purpose and excitement.

Lastly, we emphasize the importance of commitment and taking action. It's not enough to simply dream or talk about your goals; you must be committed to the journey and ready to take concrete steps toward your desired outcomes. Through proactive engagement and consistent effort, you can bring your aspirations to life and create a life that aligns with your deepest desires.

So, get ready to embrace the thrill of exploration and ignite your passion for personal growth. By examining your beliefs and values, creating a playlist, embracing your life's narrative, and committing to taking action, you are setting yourself up for a transformative and fulfilling journey ahead. Let's dive in and make the most of this incredible adventure together!

Time to Get Excited!

Not sure where I saw this video; it could have been on YouTube or another social media platform. As bad as we can talk about the negative aspects of social media, I can say it has brought me entertainment, laughter, inspiration, and so many great gems. One gem I'll never forget was a post regarding an exchange between two men who were discussing what had the highest form of value. One of guys said that he thought people, including him, would think money would be most valuable to them. He goes on to say, "I mean think about it, have you ever said, 'If I had more money I would…' or 'I wish I had more money so I could….'"?

The other man replied, "I get it. Money is indeed important." The other man then challenged him and asked while asserting what he thought to be true. "It's not even your top five, though?"

He said, "What?"

The other man responded, "No, it's not your top five." And went on to explain what he meant.

"If I say I'll give you a million dollars a day, but you got to die tomorrow, which one would you want? Would you want the money?"

"No," the first guy responded.

"So time is more valuable than money. If I say, I'll give you a million dollars a day, but you got to be sick for the rest of your life, you want it?"

"No," the guy responded.

"So health is more valuable than money. Well, if I say I'll give you a million dollars a day and your mama got to die tomorrow, you want it?"

"No," the guy responded.

"So relationships are more valuable than money. In conclusion, finances are not the highest form of value or compensation, *fulfillment* is."

This illustrates that our focus on our passion and purpose is not to make money. Yes, it is a necessity to live; however, life is bigger than money. Focus on the feeling you get when you are fulfilled, focus on the feeling you get when you are creating, impacting lives, connecting with others, living, and thriving. Lean into your life's purpose. Seize what's already yours. Get excited and enjoy the journey.

Clarity On What You're Passionate About

Working with children and families has been the core of my passion to serve. In elementary through high school and beyond, helping others seemed to be part of me. Whether it was helping someone with their homework, sharing my lunch, speaking up to defend someone, or volunteering at a safe house for trafficked survivors, helping others brings me joy. My professional career has navigated from social work to mental health and coaching. It's been a natural transition for me to help women heal from childhood trauma and limiting beliefs to getting clarity on what's important to them so they can live a full meaning and authentic life.

When I speak with my clients, they share their fears about their lives. They fear not finding true love, they fear leaving relationships that do not feel like love, and they fear not having the career they dream of and the money to live the lifestyle they desire. They fear that they can't take care of all the things they feel responsible for. The ruminating thoughts won't stop. The list goes on. So many fears but one of the most significant fears they all have in common is the fear of not knowing what their *purpose is,* and for most, this means professionally.

This is where the rubber meets the road. Our roles and positions feel important to us; however, our roles don't define us wholly. Nonetheless, we do heavily correlate our sense of self to our accomplishments and the work we do. Unsurprisingly, this happens as we spend most of our waking hours at work or working within our businesses.

For some of us, we may have found ourselves in jobs, positions, and industries that we are very much satisfied with, and for others, their work and career are the focal points of stress, worry, frustration, burnout, and unfulfillment. As I write these words, I think about how I felt exactly this way a couple of years before I finally left my job after being there for 22 years. I'll never forget the day when I knew I had to leave the agency. Working within an agency that disproportionally removed Black and brown children was wearing on me. The frustration stemmed from the feeling that no matter what new flavor of the month was being implemented, the outcomes were the same. I felt like part of the problem. I also felt anxious and overwhelmed by being micromanaged. It was so annoying, and I did not need anyone hovering and constantly following up with me. This director also had a style of asking rapid-flying questions. One day I received an email that questioned the completion of a project, in combination with a court ruling I believe was unjust, as the relative caregiver was denied the ability to have their relative placed with them and the child would remain in an unrelated home for adoption. It was more of the same for me. I had seen too many cases like this and quite frankly I was sick of it. I had moral distress. I felt the child welfare system was rooted in white supremacy. It would take me four years to leave after that moment. Yes, I had stayed far past my expiration date. For me, I had to examine the fear I had associated with leaving. This was a job that had provided me with an exceptional salary and benefits for over 22 years; I was able to be confident that every two weeks, money was hitting my account. Deep down I knew that was not my final life assignment. Once I sat with that initial discomfort, I was able to see what was on the other side. It was my freedom, my peace. Are you prepared to seize your freedom? Are you prepared to bet on yourself? Are you prepared to dream big? Do you believe in magic? Your magic?

What do you *really* want? Answer this without allowing other people's opinions or beliefs to limit you. Answer this without thinking about limitations. Imagine for a moment that money is not an issue and that whatever is currently blocking you is magically taken care of. Not sure if you believe in magic or not but consider this: There's a strategy I use with both my clients in my mental health and coaching businesses, and it's very effective in helping you figure out your true goals. It's called the "magic wand" technique. Imagine that you have a magic wand that you can wave over a particular area of your life. When you wave this magic wand, your wishes come true, and your forgotten dream will come true! Use the magic wand over your business and career. Maybe you don't believe in magic. Can you believe in yourself? Can you believe in the magic within you? Use this area to just go off and believe in magic, the magic of the wand, the magic of you.

List your magic wand wish:

_____

_____

_____

_____

_____

Did you forget something?

I am not referring to the previous exercise, I'm hinting at those lost, forgotten dreams. What are some things you wanted, desired, or dreamed about that at some point you decided you could *not* have and so you stopped wanting them? This could have been in childhood or adulthood. You may have not allowed yourself to think about these desires for a long time. For each one, ask yourself if this is something that you *still* desire. If not, cross it out and let it go. Circle any desires that you feel a strong emotional reaction to when you think about them. Again, this is not the time for your resistance to get in the way. The resistance may come in the form of a limiting belief that it is not possible.

If you could consider that all things are possible, what is it you desire?

_____

_____

_____

_____

_____

Make a list of everything important to your life. This might include:

- Particular relationships
- Being respected
- Being in good health
- Independence
- Giving time and service
- Having time to relax

- Having stimulating work
- Financial security
- Spiritual well-being
- Physical fitness
- Being an advocate for others
- Making the most of your creative talents

Make your list in order of importance. Spend some time reflecting on your list. Does what you think is important match up with the time you spend? Do you need to make some adjustments?

What's In Your Inner Being?

What do you desire? What do you desire in life? What do you desire for your life? What do you desire to create in your life? What do you desire to have in your life? What do you desire to be, *do*, and *have*? If you don't achieve this goal and desire, what will your life look like? How will you feel?

For many of us, we operate from a negative mindset and can easily say what we *don't* want rather than what we *do* want. I believe what we focus on grows so therefore when we focus on something we don't want or speak it out we are just amplifying and bringing to us that which we don't want. I have come to truly believe in the law of attraction and am very mindful of how I speak and think about things. Yet this is just something I have recently shifted in my thinking and my language. I too, previously spoke in these terms. It's so easy to focus on it because it may be the result that was painful, so I get why we are clear in our speech that we "don't" want something.

At times what we want is the opposite of what we don't want but we are not able to articulate it. To get clear on what you *do* want, we are going first to find out what you *don't* want. These can be things that you used to have in your life, and you never want that experience again. They can also be things that are currently in your life you want to stop or remove, thinking you are certain you don't want in your future. Once you list the NOT WANTS, the DO WANTS will be easier to identify. Once you get your DO WANT column completed, spend some time with each DO WANT and get present with what you are *feeling*. That's the purpose of all of this: good feelings, good vibes, and doing things that give you those good feelings and good vibes.

I Do NOT Want:	I DO Want:

You've determined some things you want and don't want. You are clear that to bring what you want more into clarity and existence, your focus will be on your DO WANTS because we are focusing on how we *feel* when we think, speak, and engage in it. You have determined the roles and beliefs that have influenced your life story and the new perspectives you can now take from them. You will feel the awakening that is happening. You'll find yourself noticing more and more things that make you think, "Yes, I want this!" and "Yes, I want more of this!" to the things you like and "No, thank you" to the things you don't like. By saying thank you, you are acknowledging that you appreciate the ability to identify what you don't want because it helps you grow and know more clearly what you *do* want.

Identify Your Core Values

Being excited about life starts with honoring what's important to you. Life is more satisfying and meaningful when it is aligned with your beliefs and values.

Below is a sample list of values. This list is only to give you ideas; this is not an exhaustive list and there's certainly room for you to add more.

Authenticity	*Adventure*	*Balance*	*Compassion*
Community	*Community*	*Determination*	*Fairness*
Faith	*Justice*	*Kindness*	*Knowledge*
Stability	*Integrity*	*Accountability*	*Courage*

Core Values

What are the most important things in your life?

1._____

2._____

3._____

4._____

5._____

What would you do with your life if you were guaranteed success?

_____

_____

_____

_____

_____

What needs would you be meeting by doing what you gave as your answer to #3?

_____

_____

_____

_____

_____

During my junior year in high school, I participated in the drama club. Reciting *Phenomenal Woman* by Maya Angelou was a highlight of my high school memories. *"I'm not cute or built to suit a fashion model's size, but when I start to tell them, they think I'm telling lies. I say, 'It's in the reach of my arms, the span of my hips, the stride of my step, the curl of my lips. I'm a woman phenomenally. Phenomenal woman, that's me.'"*

I also recited this as a candidate for the National Council of Negro Women teen pageant. I felt so empowered saying the words, not even close to being a *"woman"*. At the time I did not understand its truest meaning as a woman to love who we are and accept ourselves, flaws and all. I spent many years not loving all the parts of me. I am so grateful that my journey has led me to being the woman I am. I am the creator of my reality and so are you. If you imagine your life like a movie, you will see that you play a character in this movie. This character is a *role* that you are playing. In fact, the character has multiple roles it plays. Make a list of the roles you play in life. There are generally two categories: career and relationships. You most likely play multiple roles in the "relationship" category, such as parent, partner, child, sibling, etc. You may play more than one role under the "career" category too, such as programmer, manager, director, or CEO. If you're an entrepreneur or solopreneur, you're wearing several hats and playing many roles.

Complete these questions for each IMPORTANT role you play:

CAREER ROLES

What is your career?	
What role do you play in that career?	
What are the traits, behaviors, and qualities of a person who is playing this role "correctly"	
What are the traits, behaviors, and qualities of a person who's playing this role 'incorrectly"	
How does how YOU act out this role compare to what you believe you 'should' be doing?	
Where did you learn how to play this role?	
Do you truly believe that the definition you have identified for this role is "correct"? If not, how would you change it?	
Does it feel right for you to be playing this role the way you are playing it now? Does it feel right to be playing at all?	
How would you need to play the role differently in order for it to be in integrity with your true self?	

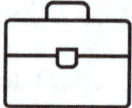

RELATIONSHIP ROLES

You will want to complete the questions below for each of the most important roles you identify.

What role do you play in your relationships?	
What are the traits, behaviors, and qualities of a person who is playing this role "correctly"?	
What are the traits, behaviors, and qualities of a person who's playing this role 'incorrectly"?	
How does how you act out this role compare to what you believe you 'should' be doing?	
Where did you learn how to play this role?	
Do you truly believe that the definition you have identified for this role is" correct"? If not, how would you change it?	
How does it feel to be playing this role? Does it feel right for you to be playing this role the way you are playing it now? Does it feel right to be playing at all?	
How would you need to play the role differently in order for it to be in integrity with your true self?	

? EMPOWERful Questions

Who, if anyone, would be affected by you letting go (or change) the roles that don't serve you?

_____

_____

_____

_____

_____

What benefit do you get from maintaining these roles the way they are?

_____

_____

_____

_____

_____

What benefits would you get from removing or changing them?

_____

_____

_____

_____

_____

Who would you be if the roles you don't want to play anymore were to disappear?

_____

_____

_____

_____

This next exercise is for you to take a closer look at your professional journey. The series of questions is designed for you to get clarity and get closer to what excites you; closer to you uncovering your passion and purpose! This may feel like you're updating your resume, but I promise it's not. You may want to reference your resume, but jotting down the first thing that comes to mind instead of a scripted answer can be very valuable as it's a reflection of your initial thoughts on the topic.

List the jobs you have had in the past and for how long. For each job, give your job title, what the role involves, and the skills and abilities it requires. Then indicate what you liked and did not like in the role. Spend some time on this part. Feel all the feels when you list your likes and dislikes.

What professional and academic qualifications do you have and what training courses have you completed?

_____

_____

_____

_____

_____

What other personal qualities, skills, or experience do you have that might be useful in a work setting? Describe and give examples of when you have demonstrated the qualities or skills or how you gained the experience.

_____

_____

_____

_____

_____

What other interests, either in a personal capacity or in work do you find interesting, or do you think you would find interesting if you had the opportunity and relevant experience/qualifications to do them?

_____

_____

_____

_____

Given your experience, qualifications/training, skills, and interests as described above, list below some possible careers or jobs that you might find out more about or apply for:

_____

_____

_____

_____

Assessing Your Next Move

If you could do any type of profession, career, or task and money, skill and time were not a concern, what would you do?

_____

_____

_____

_____

_____

What do you believe is stopping you from doing this?

_____

_____

_____

What proof do you have of this belief?

_____

_____

_____

_____

I've been asking you to answer questions and sometimes it sticks with us more when we read it as we are answering it for ourselves. Answer the next questions in first person.

If I could do one thing endlessly without getting bored or tired, what would it be? It's an activity that brings me pure delight and allows me to lose track of time whenever I engage in it.

_____

_____

_____

What kind of work do I love so much that I could do it all day long without ever feeling tired or bored? It's a task or profession that keeps me fully engaged and excited, making the concept of "work" fade away.

_____

_____

_____

_____

_____

Which activities in my work consistently provide the most abundant rewards and satisfaction in relation to the time I allocate to them? Whether it's dedicating a mere 30 seconds or a few minutes, these tasks often unveil valuable insights or foster deep connections.

_____

_____

_____

_____

_____

What is my individual superpower, a quality or skill that is completely unique to me and provides me with a special advantage in achieving success? This can be a combination of natural talent, learned skills, and personal attributes that have been developed and honed over time, and allows you to make meaningful contributions, inspire others, and achieve success in your own way.

_____

_____

_____

_____

_____

_____

Complete each sentence, don't overthink it, just the first thing that comes to mind. Read the statements out loud so the words will vibrationally resonate and inspire you.

I am most fulfilled and effective when I am:

_____

_____

_____

_____

The specific thing I do that allows me to perform at my highest level is:

_____

_____

_____

The thing that brings me the greatest joy when I'm involved in that is:

_____

_____

_____

Explore these questions and let your true passion shine through as they help you discover the type of work that truly ignites your passion and allows you to thrive with endless enthusiasm. Contemplating these questions will also help you identify the work-related activities that provide the greatest sense of abundance and satisfaction, regardless of the amount of time invested.

Sis, reflecting on these questions can help you uncover your unique abilities and understand the qualities that make you truly exceptional. Embrace your individuality and leverage your unique strengths to create a meaningful impact! There is only one you! Act like it.

YOU ARE WORTHY- YOU ARE WORTH IT

How important is living your life's purpose to you?

_____

_____

_____

_____

What can you do today to honor your life's purpose?

_____

_____

_____

_____

_____

What more might you do at this time to further your career/business?

_____

_____

_____

_____

What is currently holding you back from doing it?

_____

_____

_____

_____

_____

_____

_____

What realistically might you commit to doing now?

_____

_____

_____

_____

_____

_____

Call it my midlife awareness, because it certainly is not a crisis. However, I am aware that my time here is precious. I can't say this enough. Stop waiting. You could get hit by a bus next week. I know that sounds a bit dramatic, however, do not waste your life waiting, worrying, or wishing for things to change. You gotta want it enough. You gotta want to make it happen. After you wish for it, you gotta work for it.

Create Your Play Playlist

Some use the term 'bucket list' to indicate things to do before you 'kick the bucket' or die. We all know that our physical time here on Earth is limited. As I once heard a client say. "None of us are getting out of here alive", I interpret the phrase 'kick the bucket' as if it's a race against time before you die, and that thinking is kinda morbid. Instead of thinking about our mortality, I invite you to think about your vitality. I coined the term 'play playlist' versus 'bucket list'. A play playlist is a list of activities you want to do, goals you want to achieve, and places you want to visit in your lifetime. Ya girl is here for the fun times and enjoying myself. This past year I've been roller skating, learning Chicago stepping, been at the shooting range, hiking, rowing, kayaking, horseback riding, tea partying, white partying, paint partying, ladies' spa day, Sunday brunch and especially chilling in my She Shed aka Shebana. Big fun. Comedian Deon Cole said some of the realist shit on one of his specials. He said that we only have a certain amount of "summers" left before our time is up. When he said that, I'm telling you, something in me changed. I really felt him. I committed to have more fun because my summers were declining and "I'm outside"! Seriously creating your play playlist is about you curating your life's enjoyment.

When we were kids, 'play' was a very important aspect of our development and entertainment. When we become adults, we get so damn serious and forget about accessing that part of us. We forget to experience wonder, a feeling of surprise and admiration that we have when we see or experience something beautiful, unusual, or unexpected. Look back at the list of goals you worked on at the beginning of the book. Maybe there's a vacation or experience you have not written down yet. Remember, these are things you *really* desire to accomplish on your life's journey. It's fun to create the list by yourself and as a group activity. Who knows, maybe you can do a group play playlist trip or retreat. Make it fun. You only have one life!

Write your play playlist now.

1.

2.

3.

4.

5.

6.

7.

8.

9.

10.

11.

12.

13.

14.

15.

16.

17.

18.

19.

20.

What is stopping you from doing some of these things now?

_____

_____

_____

_____

What can you do to overcome that barrier?

_____

_____

_____

Which activity will you do first?

_____

_____

_____

What do you need to do to make it happen?

_____

_____

_____

_____

Visualization - Create A Movie

Knowing what we want in life and what our purpose is can be a gradual awakening inside; a whisper that speaks to us gently and softly. For some, the voice is louder and more discerning and may reveal itself sooner. Whatever your path, knowing your life's focus is your internal road map. When we have a map, we can get there without getting lost. Knowing your life's purpose prevents you from letting the "shoulds" should on you. Often when we think in these terms, it's likely coming from outside influences or a sense of judgment on ourselves. Let your 'shoulds' become desires. Knowing *your* purpose keeps you from comparing yourself to others. This is your life, what are you going to make of it?

When I worked for Alameda County there was a voice inside my head that said, "Renee, you could just continue working here until you're ready to retire and collect your pension in your 60s. You're a leader here, you can advance more or even stay here at this senior management position." That was the message we got from our parents: Get your education or learn a trade and get a good job so you can retire. In my case, I had a "good government job". Yet, when I got that "good government job", I told myself I wasn't going to work for "the man" longer than five years. However, as I indicated, I found purpose in advocating for relative placements and still, there was a part of me that knew this was not going to be my final career destination. I was shifting my career focus as my mental health practice expanded and took off. I began to see my impact in other ways. I paid attention to how I felt when I was doing the work. I felt inspired and empowered while supporting these women. When I decided to start my private practice and coaching exclusively, it was a relief off my shoulders that I had been carrying. I leaned into the mindset that I was no longer settling for anything less than what I desired and what I deserved.

I'm no longer ignoring my heart's calling. I'm no longer playing small. I'm permitting myself to step into the highest, most authentic, most abundant version of myself.

My Movie, My Life

Imagine that tomorrow morning you wake up and suddenly find that a magical transformation, a miracle, has taken place! Your world is just as you would like it to be, and you have resolved all your problems and have come to terms with all the things that were bothering you. *Describe what is different and what the particular things are that tell you that things have changed. Enter as much detail as you can.*

_____

_____

_____

_____

_____

_____

_____

_____

_____

_____

_____

_____

_____

What can you do that would help you move towards My Movie, My Life you have described, even if it's in a small way?

_____

_____

_____

_____

_____

_____

_____

_____

What can you do that would result in a massive impact on My Movie, My Life you have described?

_____

_____

_____

_____

_____

_____

_____

_____

Commit To a Smart Action Plan

Goals get me going. Once I put a goal in the vortex, it comes to fruition. Well, I can't flippantly say *all* my goals because there have been some personal goals that haven't panned out. This would be my two marriages. In each, the goal was "till death do us part" yet, my divorce decrees represent lessons. I previously would think of it as a "failed" goal. However, the shifting of my perspectives has allowed me to embrace that part of my journey and look for the lessons learned. The next chapter spills the tea on the love and relationship lessons learned.

At the beginning of this book, I urged you to think about what's important to you and write your mission statement. Perhaps you may feel a bit clearer and closer to the vision of your purpose. Maybe you are already living it and you have more goals to accomplish because you have so much you want to offer this world, and Sis, I'm telling you, the world needs your impact!

As you know, having a plan is key. But before you work on the plan, there must be the idea, the goal, in mind. Let yourself immerse in the delightful feelings of crushing your goals and the delightful feeling of *the feeling*. Feel the feels. Even the uncomfortable part.

Great goals are:

a) Outcome-focused: Once you understand our *why* (and it's enthusiastic *why*) you're 90% there!

b) Aligned with your values: The more the goal aligns with your inner core values, the *easier* it will be to achieve. NOTE: We can achieve goals that don't align with our values but it's harder to do and less satisfying.

c) Stated in the positive: i.e. "I want healthy eating habits" rather than "I want to stop eating fast food."

I'm sure you have heard of the acronym SMART. If you haven't, it stands for (there are a few different variations)

Specific (Do you know exactly what you're trying to achieve?)

Measurable (Do you know when you've achieved it?)

Achievable (Do you have the resources and time needed to achieve the goal?)

Relevant (Does it align with your values and long-term goals?), and

Time frame (Does it have a specific time deadline?)

Focusing On the Outcome

What is it that you really desire? Dig deep....

_____

_____

_____

_____

_____

_____

What is the specific outcome you're looking for?

_____

_____

_____

_____

_____

_____

What is the pain for you not achieving your goal?

_____

_____

_____

_____

Aligning With Your Values

Is this goal aligned with your life/vision life plan? (Don't know? What does your gut tell you?)

_____

_____

_____

Is the goal aligned with your values? Ask yourself what's really important to you in life. Will this goal help you achieve more of that?)

_____

_____

_____

Are the goals something you truly want, or are they something you think you should have or should be doing? (Tip: If it's a "should", it may be someone else's dream….)

_____

_____

_____

When you think about your goal, does it give you a sense of deep contentment or 'rightness', happiness, and/or excitement? (if so, these are good signs that it's a healthy goal.)

_____

_____

_____

How does the goal fit into your life/lifestyle? (time/effort/commitments - what else might be impacted?)

_____

_____

_____

_____

Committed To That Action

This last section is where the rubber hits the road. It's about your inspired action. If you're anything like me, you love a challenge, and completing trainings, workbooks, and workshops are fun and interesting to pursue. Is it only me who has collected and completed all these things and did not necessarily apply the learning? That was the old me, as I now take my time very seriously and I'm not doing anything that does not get used or applied to my life; everything has a reason and purpose.

Achieving goals takes commitment; commitment is a mindset, a personal value. Commitment is connected to your why. Commitment does not let setbacks deter you. Commitment looks like action once the plan has been devised. Planning requires getting barriers out of the way so you can just go without any distractions.

Identifying Obstacles

Can you start and maintain this goal/outcome? (i.e. do you have complete control over achieving it?) How will making this change affect other aspects of your life? (i.e. What else might you need to deal with?)

_____

_____

_____

_____

_____

_____

What's good about your current situation?

_____

_____

_____

_____

_____

How can you keep those aspects while still making the change?

_____

_____

_____

_____

_____

What might you have to give up/stop doing to achieve this goal? (Essentially, what's the price of making this change- are you willing to pay it?)

_____

_____

_____

_____

Who will you have to be to achieve this goal?

_____

_____

_____

_____

Goal Sizing

Is the goal the right size to be working on? Is it too big? Break it down into smaller goals. Is it too small? Fit it into a larger goal.

What would be the minimum level/super easy goal to achieve?

_____

_____

_____

What would be your target level of a goal to achieve?

_____

_____

_____

_____

_____

What would be an extraordinary level of goal to achieve?

_____

_____

_____

_____

_____

Resources - Get Moving

What resources do you already have to help you achieve your goal? Make a list (e.g. things, support from people, contacts, personal qualities, knowledge, skills, money, time, etc.)

1.

2.

3.

4.

5.

What resources do you need to help you achieve your goal?

1.

2.

3.

4.

5.

Ask yourself what outcomes you would like to achieve in the next three to six months. The word "outcome' refers to a change in your feelings, your quality of life, or relationship or satisfaction in a particular area.

Write down 1-3 important outcomes that you would like to move towards:

-

-

-

Now for each outcome you have listed above, set yourself a personal goal that meets the SMART requirements above that you want to aim to achieve within a specified time, which you believe will help you towards the outcome:

Specific	Measurable	Achievable	Relevant	Timeframe

Finally, list below the actions that you will start within the next week to help you start to move toward each goal. For each action, specify what it is, when you will do it, and which goal it is relevant to:

Action	Type of Action	When You Will Complete It	Which Goal It Is Relevant To

You've done a lot of inner work. Now after seeing your values, talents, strengths, and passions, what did you determine your life has been preparing you for?

_____

_____

_____

In what ways are you not currently living up to this greater purpose and mission in your life?

_____

_____

_____

_____

_____

What do you need to learn more about or practice in order to use your gifts and go for your dreams?

_____

_____

_____

Staying On Track

I used to say, "It's me against me" before I had the mindset shift of being in harmony with my greater self. Achieving your goals is not about you against you. It's you *with* you. Here are some ways to foolproof your goals.

Avoid doing tasks that require longer than one hour, unless absolutely necessary. If the task is challenging, explore whether breaking it down into manageable chunks would help. For example, "practice yoga" can be chunked down to "practice a yoga pose for five minutes."

Longer tasks can utilize the Pomodoro Method, long version (e.g. "Spend 45 minutes researching opportunities on LinkedIn"). Remember to be flexible and give yourself grace. Sometimes tasks take longer than anticipated. Take a deep breath and swivel, Sis. Things can be modified, spread out, or combined with something else. Protect your time, and by that, I mean protect the time that you schedule for your tasks and restorative tasks. Be mindful of your environment and remove any distractions.

We live in an era of distractions. The pings and dings are constant. Is yours Facebook? TikTok or Instagram? Email checking? Continuous messaging with friends and family? True confession about when I knew I needed an intervention: There's a feature on the iPhone that tells you how many times you picked up your phone in a day. I think my number was 177…pretty excessive, right?! Here's a strategy that works for me. I just stopped checking them so often and started batching these types of activities. Set a time, then check and deal with all of them at once. Give yourself 30 minutes and then get back on task. Ask friends not to call you at specific times. Ask them to help you stick to your schedule. Put yourself in a distraction-free mode. I love the do-not-disturb mode. My sister knows how to break through, but most will accept the straight-to-voicemail treatment. Try it, it's quite dreamy. It's like the time before we had phones.

Begin building habits that help you eliminate distractions and stay focused. Start by creating an environment in which you're less tempted to get preoccupied with something other than what you're working on. This isn't always easy to do. For one, many of us rely on a computer to do our work, but we also find our biggest distractions enabled by the use of a computer on the internet. If you constantly find yourself wandering over to videos or shopping websites, (stop stalking me Amazon!), try using a website blocker app. Monitor your mind-wandering.

Removing clutter also helps. We spend nearly 50 percent of our waking time thinking about something other than what we're supposed to be doing, according to one Harvard study. (https://news.harvard.edu/gazette/story/2010/11/wandering-mind-not-a-happy-mind/)

We are on autopilot and our minds are wandering, in part to avoid the effort of focusing on something. The key to heightened productivity is to notice when your mind's distracted and bring your attention back to task.

It's like meditation and mindfulness, just gently bringing yourself back into focus. Here's the thing, most of us spend far too much time on things that ultimately do not matter (what our hair looks like today) or that we do not have control over (worrying about the future). We have the choice at every moment to choose where we put our energy and attention. We get to choose what we want every moment and how we want to live our lives, moment by moment. How you manage your time is up to you. What type of goals you create for yourself is up to you. Time is a resource. How you spend it is up to you and it has an impact. Are you making SMART choices? Are your goals SMART?

Now you have the strategies to get clarity on what matters to you and how to get into massive action. Faith is dead without work, so it's critically important to be committed to taking action in pursuit of your goals and aspirations. That commitment is the driving force that propels you forward, transforming your dreams into reality. By understanding and embracing the power of commitment, you can overcome obstacles, maintain focus, and ultimately achieve success.

Recognize that commitment is a mindset, a conscious decision to follow through on our intentions, regardless of the challenges we may encounter along the way. The distinction between mere interest and genuine commitment is understanding that commitment requires unwavering dedication, perseverance, and a willingness to go the extra mile.

By embracing commitment as a guiding principle in your life, you can overcome obstacles, stay focused, and ultimately realize your aspirations. It is through commitment that we unlock our true potential and create a life of purpose and meaning. So let us embrace commitment wholeheartedly, for it is the pathway to our greatest successes.

I bet you didn't know this - there are 1,440 minutes in each day. But today, you can walk away knowing and feeling empowered that you get to decide how much balance, wellness, and success you get to have in your life. *You* get to determine the amount of joy and abundance you have in your life. I don't know about you, but that really excites me! I invite you to get excited, make time, and live *your* life!

Are you reaching toward wellness and balance for yourself? That is my greatest hope - that the words from this book inspire you to create a life of wellness.

EMPOWER

CHAPTER 8

Relationships - Offering Yourself

Many of us are conditioned to think of a relationship in a "WIIFM mentality", or *What's In It For Me*. I certainly have. Quite frankly, I believe that it's really part of our socialization and biology. In the womb, our needs were met, and as infants and children, our basic needs were met. Unfortunately, for some of us that may not be the case, which has other ramifications, such as being emotionally unavailable or drawn to emotionally unavailable people. Have you ever felt like you're getting the short end of the stick in a relationship? Have you ever felt like being in a relationship is the most fulfilling experience you've ever had? I certainly have felt the gamut.

Relationships are one of the most important "things" you'll do in your life. I have come to believe that the relationship with self is most important. How you treat yourself and how you feel about yourself will be the pillar of how you show up in your relationships. When you feel good about yourself and have a self-awareness about what you like and don't like, who you are, how you want to 'be', how you want to be treated, and how you want to 'be' towards others, you're able to:

* Set healthy boundaries and communicate your needs and desires effectively.

* Make choices that align with your values and goals.

* Build strong, positive relationships based on mutual respect and trust.

* Advocate for yourself and others respectfully and assertively.

* Embrace your uniqueness and celebrate diversity in others.

* Practice self-care and prioritize your mental, emotional, and physical well-being.

* Cultivate a strong sense of self-worth and self-acceptance, which can lead to greater

happiness and success in all areas of life.

I have contemplated this final chapter for many years. I have wondered to myself, "How much are you going to reveal?" I felt this part of my life was very personal and downright embarrassing. Yet, that is my ego telling me that I should be ashamed of my relationship outcomes. My second marriage and divorce have taught me more about myself and have brought me to the point of recognizing the true meaning of self-love and prioritizing my peace.

In my private practice, some of my clients have shared their fears and frustrations with both being in relationships and dating. Just to be clear, all the relationship concerns aren't just "romantic" types, they are also relationships with mothers, fathers, sisters, brothers, etc. One client, "Jasmine", came to therapy seeking support in coping with her feelings of depression and anxiety. She was finding it increasingly hard to manage. She was preoccupied with the feelings and worries she had regarding her mother, who had subjected her to abuse and neglect. Her mother did drugs, so they lived an unstable life. She even recalled living in their car for long periods, in addition to a shelter, motels, and couch surfing with friends and relatives. She recalled her mother being distant and cold towards her, along with lots of criticism and harsh words of disappointment. She does not recall her mother ever showing affection in any way, and hugging was foreign to her. Fast forward to now, and she is faced with caring for her mother as her health and mental capacity has declined significantly. Through therapy, Jasmine began to understand the impact of her childhood experiences on her mental health and well-being. She learned to recognize how her mother's abuse and neglect had shaped her beliefs and behaviors, and how it had influenced her relationships with others. With my support, Jasmine began to work through her feelings of anger, hurt, and guilt and developed healthier coping skills to manage her emotions.

As Jasmine continued in therapy, she began to see the irony in the fact that she was now caring for the same mother who neglected and abused her. However, through our work together, she was able to reframe this situation as an opportunity for healing and growth. Jasmine realized that she was not only caring for her mother but also for the wounded child within herself.

With a newfound sense of self-awareness and compassion, Jasmine was able to approach her mother's care with a sense of empathy and understanding. She was able to set healthy boundaries and communicate her needs and concerns effectively, while still ensuring that her mother received the care and support she needed.

In the end, Jasmine's therapy journey helped her to heal from the wounds of her past and find a sense of peace and closure. She was able to develop a more positive sense of self and build stronger, healthier relationships with others. Jasmine's journey has been one of transformation and growth, and it has been a privilege to witness her healing and resilience.

The complex relationship between my male clients and their mothers can be equally painful and difficult to navigate. A dysfunctional mother-son relationship can be characterized by a lack of communication, trust, and respect. When a mother is unsupportive or critical of her son, it can lead to feelings of inadequacy, low self-esteem, and resentment. The son may struggle to communicate his needs and feelings to his mother, leading to a feeling of disconnection and isolation. The son may also feel the need to constantly please his mother to gain her approval and validation, but his efforts may be met with criticism and rejection. This can further damage the relationship, leading to a cycle of guilt, resentment, and frustration for both parties. One male client of mine, "Lance", shares his frustration with his mother and has developed the ability to set boundaries. He has recognized that he does not have to participate in the drama with her. He is also aware that the dynamic that he has with his mother also plays out in his intimate relationships. He has gained a deeper awareness that he has been drawn to the same type of woman his mother is: critical, dismissive, and emotionally unavailable.

Through therapy, Lance was able to recognize the patterns of behavior that he had developed in response to his mother's criticism and emotional unavailability. He realized that he had been unconsciously seeking out relationships that mirrored the dynamics of his childhood, perpetuating a cycle of hurt and disappointment.

With my support, Lance began to break free from this cycle by setting boundaries with his mother and developing healthier communication patterns. He learned to recognize the signs of emotional unavailability in his romantic partners and took steps to avoid repeating the same patterns in his relationships. He was able to reframe his experiences and develop a deeper understanding of himself and his needs. Lance's journey has been one of self-discovery and empowerment. He has learned to break free from the patterns of his past and cultivate healthier, more fulfilling relationships.

The irony of Lance's situation was not lost on him. He had spent years trying to win his mother's approval and love, only to realize that he had been chasing after the wrong kind of love all along. But with the help of therapy, he was able to reframe his experiences and develop a deeper understanding of himself and his needs.

Lance's story highlights the importance of self-awareness and boundary-setting in breaking free from the patterns of our past. With the help of therapy, we can gain a deeper understanding of ourselves and develop the tools we need to build healthier, more fulfilling relationships.

In my journey and through the lives of others, it is my opinion that we are here to connect with others, in community and in love. In this chapter, you will uncover the secrets to creating and experiencing meaningful relationships. Listen, I'm not Steve Harvey or a relationship expert. These practices and principles are based on a belief and value system. Therefore, everything is not for everyone. I believe mastering these secrets will allow you to claim the type of relationship you dream about. When you master your mindset, you can be *intentional,* and your life will be so much richer.

There is a caveat, however; everything we intend to happen does not always necessarily happen. I certainly *intended* on having my happily ever after and at this juncture of my journey I've realized my happily ever after does not have anything to do with my marital status or my role at a job. My happiness starts with *me*. Yet, experiencing our lives in community with others and experiencing love is greatest when we give ourselves, as a gift of love from our overflow.

I am a lover of discovering ways to improve my communication, and many years ago I had the pleasure of being introduced to *The Four Agreements*. *The Four Agreements* are a set of self-help principles developed by Don Miguel Ruiz. They are intended to help individuals develop a more positive outlook on life and break free from negative cycles of thinking and behavior. I believe that *The Four Agreements* can be beneficial in creating a standard for themselves as it relates to engaging in relationships, partnerships, and friendships.

The Four Agreements are:

1. Be impeccable with your word

2. Don't take anything personally

3. Don't make assumptions, and

4. Always do your best

Seems pretty straightforward, right? Very commonsensical, would you agree? I can't help but think about a big snag in my last marriage when I think about the first agreement, *Be impeccable with your word*. My ex-husband would tell me that I tricked him and lied to him to get him to marry me. When he said those things, I felt deeply hurt. When we were dating, I would eagerly cook for him. A ribeye steak with a veggie was his favorite and he could get it at all hours. I would get up and make it for him or have it waiting for him upon his arrival, even booty-call hours. I knew getting a meal prepared for him was his love language. He was accustomed to getting his meals prepared, still, by his mother, which included her making his plate and bringing it to him. I had no problem with cooking and making and bringing him his plate; it made me feel good that he enjoyed my cooking.

However, over the years, I became resentful because of my unmet needs and his harsh and critical treatment of me during the marriage. I was no longer inspired to cook and serve him. In some ways, I will admit, I did change. I did not *happily* cook and serve him anymore. I can't blame him and say he changed me, but bit by bit, each experience and interaction changed and tugged at me until I was a shell of myself. The following is an examination of Don Miguel Ruiz's *Four Agreements*

1. Be Impeccable with Your Word

Speak with integrity and honesty. Say what you mean and mean what you say. This agreement asks us to use our words carefully and to refrain from speaking against ourselves or others or using blame or judgment. Speak with integrity. Say only what you mean. Avoid using your words to speak against yourself or others. Use the power of your words to grow truth and love.

 *EMPOWERul Questions*

How has my lack of clarity impacted relationships in the past?

_____

_____

_____

_____

Where do I over-commit or over-promise?

_____

_____

How can I be more honest with myself?

_____

_____

_____

How do I use sarcasm in ways that are not clear or honest?

_____

_____

_____

Where do my boundaries need clarification?

_____

_____

_____

_____

2. Don't Take Anything Personally

Take responsibility for your own thoughts and feelings and remember that what others do is not because of you. Realize that nothing others do is because of you, but instead a projection of their own reality, self-work, and dreams. When you are immune to the opinions and actions of others, it will free you from needless suffering. In the mental health field, this is actually a "coping" response, a negative, automatic response. Personalization is one of many ways we respond to and interpret information.

In life, we have control over our response, how we internalize something, etc. We are not able to grow until we slow down, get quiet, get honest, and reflect on our participation in the mess. In lots of cases, we are participating in the mess because we let others' opinions and judgments fuck with us. I will speak personally for myself. My ex-husband would say some downright foul, demeaning, disrespectful, abusive, and hurtful things to me. I would try to figure out what I did to deserve that treatment. My feelings would be so hurt, and over time I became numb to the attacks. Before the numbness, I internalized the insults. I felt like I was not enough. I constantly heard from him, "You're the one with the problem, not me." Ouch.

Many of us take what people say to us to heart. Have you ever let something someone said to you make you feel bad, and you couldn't stop thinking about it, and you were consumed with the conversation or interaction?

EMPOWERful Questions

What situations do I take things most personally?

_____

_____

_____

_____

_____

How am I projecting my own insecurities onto others?

_____

_____

_____

_____

What helps me be immune to the opinions of others?

_____

_____

_____

_____

How has taking things personally impacted my relationships?

_____

_____

_____

_____

_____

I get how it may be difficult to "not" take an insult or verbal attack personally. At the end of the day other people's opinions are *their* business, their lens and perspectives and really, they have a right to their opinion. You, on the other hand, don't have to agree with it or entertain it. The more you can grasp this concept, the freer you can go through life open with your love and free of fear of judgment and rejection.

3. Don't Make Assumptions

Be careful not to write the 'back script' on what others say or do. We love to "create" a story. We, as humans, need to know what something "means". This will cause us to fill in the blanks because our "meaning-making machine" won't turn off. Instead of jumping to a "story", find the courage to ask questions to prevent misunderstandings and communication breakdowns.

A client of mine, who has been married for over two decades, shared a story of assumptions that almost turned into a big conflict and misunderstanding. Luckily, information was revealed to prevent her from driving the car off the cliff, but her assumptions had her feeling pissed the hell off. She overheard her husband on the phone about a hotel reservation, but he didn't mention anything about it when he got off the phone. She walked around festering that he was up to something. He later told her he would be home at noon the next day and she even scheduled it in her phone to cuss him out at that exact opportune time. But as the old saying goes, when you make an assumption, you make an ass of u and me (ass/u/me). When she went to schedule the time to cuss him out and to tell him all the other unsavory things she had on her mind, her calendar revealed she and her husband had plans to go out of town, plans they actually had made six months prior. Yet her negative assumptions had her in a totally different head space. What she was assuming was false.

This is common for us folks. Sometimes it's a trauma response and other times it's just a cognitive response. Have you ever made an assumption, but you were totally wrong, and you had the negative emotions to match the inaccurate assumption? Ask questions and communicate as clearly as you can about misunderstandings, sadness, and drama. Have the courage to express what you really want. Stay curious about yourself and others around you to create room to honor your individuality and growth.

 ## EMPOWERful Questions

When is it easier for me to ask for help?

_____

_____

_____

What helps me circle back and check in when there has been a miscommunication?

_____

_____

_____

Where do I most frequently get caught in assumption-making?

_____

_____

_____

How has making up stories served me? How has it impacted my relationships negatively?

_____

_____

_____

_____

4. Always Do Your Best

When you do your best, you can avoid negative self-judgment, regret, guilt, and shame. Doing your best allows you to present your healthiest self in relationships with others. Doing your best most importantly allows you to present a sense of wellness to yourself.

Doing my best has been easy for me. I believe it has been my trauma response to be an overachiever. I developed a hyper-focused need to rely on myself because I felt like I couldn't trust the adults in my life, and I needed to do well so I could be seen and loved. I now recognize this is an unhealthy perspective and motivation to do well. I now am inspired to do my best because of the feeling I create by doing my best. I feel a sense of pride, happiness, joy, accomplishment, fulfillment, inspiration, satisfaction, and peace within. Your best will change from moment to moment (with your health, energy, and experience) but by investing in the best of yourself you'll avoid self-judgment and regret. I love an artist named Toni Jones, if you're not familiar with her check her out, she's a total vibe. She has a song called 'Worth Ethic' and the line…'I'm not a Perfectionist, I'm an Excellentist' and that's where I live now.

 *EMPOWERful Questions*

Where can I show up more authentically in my life?

_____

_____

_____

_____

_____

What will help me be brave enough to be vulnerable and put my best out there?

_____

_____

_____

_____

_____

How will I know when I am really doing my best?

_____

_____

_____

How will I draw a line between doing my best and doing too much?

_____

_____

_____

Where do I most easily bring my best self? What can that experience tell me about bringing my best in the future?

_____

_____

_____

By incorporating these *Four Agreements* into your relationships with family, friends, and colleagues, you are setting the stage for healthy communication and positive relationships.

Identify Your Love Language and The Four Horsemen

Love is a language and fortunately for us, there are several different dialects. The key is knowing how you receive and feel loved. Equally as important is knowing the love language of other important people in your life and the ability to recognize it when interacting with others.

Love language is not just about romantic connections, and understanding love languages can have a profound impact on all your relationships. A partner, a parent, a child, a sibling, or a friend can all have different needs and roles in your life and they too, experience love differently.

Here are the five love languages. They are not in any particular order.

Words of Affirmation. Saying: "I love you", "You're amazing", and "I'm so lucky to have you in my life."

Learning the reasons behind someone's affection can elevate your mood and leave you feeling uplifted and inspired. On the other hand, criticism can have a lasting negative impact and be difficult to shake off. Positive, supportive, and encouraging words, however, can have a profoundly uplifting effect on one's spirit and well-being.

Acts of Service. Actions speak louder than words. Anything you do to ease the burden of responsibilities weighing on an "Acts of Service" person will speak volumes. You feel delighted when someone offers to assist you, whether it's a small or significant task. However, it's hurtful when someone fails to follow through on their commitments, makes empty promises, or creates more work for you instead of being helpful.

• **Receiving Gifts.** Little tokens of love and affection make you smile all day. The receiver of gifts thrives on the love, thoughtfulness, and effort behind the gift. The gift or gesture shows that you are seen and cared for. Events like birthdays and anniversaries are opportunities for thoughtful gifts, including everyday gestures. Gifts are visual representations of love and are appreciated greatly.

Quality Time. Time is valuable, and you want to spend it with your significant other. Being there for this type of person is critical, but *really* being there, with the TV off, fork and knife down, cell phone down, and all chores and tasks on standby, makes your significant other feel truly special and loved. Distractions, postponed dates, or the failure to listen can be especially hurtful. Quality time also means sharing quality conversations and quality activities.

Physical Touch. Hugging, cuddling, and holding hands is how you express your love. Physical touch is not all about sex, yet you may be more of a touchy, feely person. Hugs, back massages, hand holding, and gentle touches on the shoulder, arm, leg, or face – they can all be ways to show concern, care, and love. Physical presence and accessibility are very important, while neglect or abuse can be unforgivable and destructive. Physical touch fosters a sense of security and belonging in any relationship.

It seems quite normal to love others the way we want to be loved and our efforts may fall short of acknowledgment, and they can then lead to (mis)communication. As a result, what might appear as unappreciative is really not that at all. However, when we are aware of our needs, we are able to ask for those needs to be tended to. You will also have an indication if it's not being tended to as the feeling of being loved may feel absent. For me, I have determined that my primary love language is Words of Affirmation. However, I am aware that the need for validation from others is the slippery slope of internalizing what others say, especially if it is from someone important in your life like a partner or parent, I believe that's why I felt so much pain in my last marriage. Criticism, belittling, and dismissiveness are on the opposite spectrum of words of affirmation.

On the other hand, he spoke a love language that I least felt impacted by - gifts. He showered me with gifts. He prided himself on providing for his family. I really appreciated that about him. I could rely on him to take care of business financially. He liked buying "things" and at times it would be expensive items as his way of apologizing for some disturbance between us, and other times it would be things he knew I liked like a Reese's Peanut Butter Cup. On the flip side in my first marriage, my ex was the King of Compliments. He had the gift to gab and was full of flattery. He spoke my love language, but he also spoke a few other dialects like chronic unemployment, unreliability, and dishonesty.

Here are some benefits of knowing your love language:

1. *A deeper sense of emotional connection.* When the important people in our lives can love us in a way that resonates with us, it just feels so good. It also feels good to respond to your partner's needs.

2. *A greater self-awareness.* It helps you to understand why certain actions or words of affirmation mean more to you than others.

3. *It helps improve your communication.* Knowing your language can help you better understand how to better express your love and appreciation to your partner.

4. *It strengthens your relationships.* When both partners understand each other's love language, it creates a stronger bond and connection within the relationship.

5. *Fewer misunderstandings.* Knowing your love language can help to prevent misunderstandings and arguments due to miscommunication.

6. *Increased intimacy.* Understanding your partner's love language can help you better meet their emotional needs leading to increased intimacy.

Be mindful that you can have a healthy relationship with a partner who does not have the same love language as yours. It's probably unlikely you both have the same love language. It might require some extra effort to communicate and express your love in ways that your partner understands, but it is possible. You both must be intentional in trying to meet that need for each other. It starts with the willingness to understand and communicate to express it. It's time to take the test to see what your primary love language is www.5lovelanguages.com/quizzes/

Now that you've taken the quiz, what is your primary love language? You may have scored very close to another language and that is certainly a reality for many of us. Love can be experienced in different ways. Rank the languages.

List your primary love language:

_____

List your second love language:

_____

What is your lowest-scoring language?

_____

Who will you share this information with?

_____

What would you like to happen as a result of sharing this information?

_____

Describe a time when you experienced being loved in your primary love language.

_____

_____

_____

_____

Is It Me? I Think It's You

When we are in communication with others it's easy to point out what the other person is 'doing" or 'not doing' and we often have blind spots as it relates to our own behavior. To grow deeper connections with others, being mindful of our part in the interaction takes the mindset shift of offering yourself. Being divorced twice, I have some experience with healthy and unhealthy communication. I have lots of personal stories and stories from my friends and clients. When I worked with couples in my private practice the number one complaint was communication and a lack of intimacy. One of the resources I offered them was helping them see how "The Four Horsemen", a term coined by couples' therapist, John Gottman, were getting in the way of their intimacy and connection with each other. The Four Horseman, as Dr. Gottman suggests, are four toxic types of communication. These four horsemen can show up in all types of relationships. The couples with the most success were able to recognize their contribution to the problem and maintain a commitment to shift the way they thought about each other and the way they talked to and treated each other.

I noticed the red flags very early in both of my marriages. If I am candid with myself, they were there when we were dating, I just refused to call a spade a spade. But in my second marriage, I really questioned myself. *Why* did I ignore and minimize what I was seeing and experiencing? In the early stages of my mental health career, I read all sorts of books and academic journals. In addition, I read books on marriage because I wanted all the tools and strategies to ensure the success of my second marriage. As I read through the chapters, I quietly felt an unsettling sense that my marriage was in trouble before it really got started. My second ex-husband and I were friends before we got married. He was my homie, lover, and friend in college, and I freely shared things about myself and my past. He knew my good, bad, and ugly. Sadly, he would later weaponize things he knew about to put me down. For instance, he would tell me, "Something is wrong with you because you came from a broken home", or "Your mama's a hoe, so you're a hoe." Things he would say were actually embarrassing. When I reflect back, I'm like wow, you really let him talk and treat you like that?

I've stopped beating myself up, blaming myself for staying, and feeling guilty and ashamed about it. Instead of asking myself "why?" I ask with compassion and love, "What happened, Renee? What happened in your life that impacted you on a subconscious level that it was okay for you to be treated in that manner?" Of course, it goes back to my childhood, the fear of rejection and abandonment, and the need for validation, acceptance, and approval. In hindsight, The Four Horsemen were in plain view. My ex was hyper-critical and expressed contempt for me with his vicious putdowns. I often responded with defensiveness and we both stonewalled each other.

Below is the breakdown of the four horsemen and follow-up questions for you to consider.

1. Criticism

When you criticize your partner or a person you are implying that there is something wrong with them. Using the words, "you always" or "you never" are common ways to criticize. Your partner is most likely to feel under attack and respond defensively. This is a dangerous pattern to get into because neither person feels heard and both may begin to feel bad about themselves in the presence of the other. The antidote to criticism is to make a direct complaint that is not a global attack on your partner's or the other person's personality.

- Am I attacking the person instead of highlighting the behavior?
- Am I criticizing my partner instead of listening to them?
- Am I dismissing my partner's feelings or invalidating their point of view?

2. Contempt

Contempt is any statement or nonverbal behavior that puts you on a higher ground than your partner or another person. I consider it criticism of the 5th power. Mocking your partner or others, calling them names, rolling your eyes, and sneering in disgust are all examples of contempt. Of all the horsemen, contempt is the most serious. Couples have to realize that these types of put-downs will destroy the fondness and admiration between them. The antidote to contempt is to lower your tolerance for contemptuous statements and behaviors and to actively work on building a culture of appreciation in the relationship.

- Am I using sarcasm or contempt to belittle my partner?

- Am I blocking my partner's attempt to connect with me?

Yes, the physical attacks were devastating and traumatic, yet it was the dismissiveness and the bullying I experienced that broke me down the most. I too engaged in this horseman through the guise of sarcasm. I would be quick-witted and snarky. One friend described me as *flippant* years ago. Yes, I can let loose, and it has not been pretty when that part of me shows up. That was 'Nay Nay', and she has grown in many ways and has emotional intelligence now. Self-awareness is constant work.

3. Defensiveness:

When you attempt to defend yourself from a perceived attack with a counter complaint you are being defensive. Another way to be defensive is to whine like an innocent victim. Unfortunately, defensiveness keeps partners from taking responsibility for problems and escalates negative communication. Even if your partner is criticizing you, defensiveness is not the way to go. It will only fuel a bad exchange. The antidote to defensiveness is to try to hear your partner's or others' complaints and to take some responsibility for the problem.

- Am I being defensive or trying to shift blame onto my partner?

- Am I trying to control the conversation or manipulate my partner?

This was my issue big time. I had a problem with feedback ever since I could remember. When I heard the feedback, what I heard was, "Something is wrong with you", "You're not good enough", "You're not worthy", or "You're not smart enough." My ANTs, cognitive distortions, filtering, and personalization just couldn't take the hit. Call me fragile and sensitive, but my feelings felt crushed. I have been able to recognize that those crushed feelings came as a response to those psychologically terrible verbal attacks. But my defensiveness, as I stated, had been a long-standing issue. My first ex-husband would tease me about my resistance to feedback. He called me Evillene the Witch from the movie, *The Wiz*, because of her infamous song *"Don't Nobody Bring Me No Bad News"*. In my growing and gaining greater self-awareness, I recognize that feedback can be valuable. When I worked for Alameda County, Faith Battles, a division director, would say "Feedback is a gift." I always appreciated that belief. I'm not saying all feedback is constructive or kind, but the gift is in your ability to use it for the growth and expansion of yourself. Even things that can seem destructive and traumatic can bring about great transformation.

4. **Stonewalling:**

Stonewalling happens when the listener withdraws from the conversation. The stonewaller might physically leave, or they might just stop tracking the conversation and appear to shut down. The stonewaller may look like they don't care but that usually isn't the case. Typically, they are overwhelmed and are trying to calm themselves. Unfortunately, this seldom works because one partner is likely to assume the other partner doesn't care enough about the problem to talk about it. It can be a vicious circle with one person demanding to talk and the other looking for an escape. The antidote is to learn to identify the signs that you or your partner is starting to feel emotionally overwhelmed and to agree together to take a break. If the problem still needs to be discussed, then pick it up when you are calmer.

- Am I avoiding difficult conversations or refusing to talk about certain topics?

- Am I using anger or aggression to intimidate or threaten my partner?

In my last marriage, my ex-husband would initially retreat, ignore, or leave when we had the smallest of conflicts. It became toxic, *clap on, clap off, the Clapper* dance we would do. Then he would reengage, and we acted like nothing happened. We just swept it under the rug until the next time. Later in the marriage, I became a stonewaller. I used avoidance to keep the peace. I filled myself up with activities, business pursuits, fitness pursuits, and community service. I found in my private practice this is very common. We fill up our lives with things to do when we feel broken, hurt, unloved, and unappreciated. Does this sound familiar? Have you found things to use as a distraction when trying to avoid a person?

#RelationshipGoals Means Healthy Communication

Awareness of how you're responding, and exploration of alternative behaviors are key to improving your communication for your current relationship or future relationships. Are healthy relationships the ultimate goal? YES? Can you say #RelationshipGoals? If the goal is to improve your relationships, remember it starts with *you*.

Outcomes

List below one or more outcomes that you would like to aim to reach in respect to a particular relationship that you and the other person agree would represent an improvement in the relationship. Some examples are:

- For both of us to feel more relaxed in the relationship

- To be able to discuss things calmly rather than yelling at each other

- More quality time together

The outcome or outcomes that I would like are:

_____

_____

_____

_____

One Change in Behavior or Thought Pattern

Indicate below *one* change in either the way that you often behave (or are currently behaving) or in your pattern of thinking that you feel would help you to move towards the main outcome or outcomes above:

_____

_____

_____

_____

Benefits and Drawbacks

As discussed in the previous chapters, when people are finding it hard to make a change in a habitual behavior or thought pattern, it is often because for them the perceived drawbacks of change are nearly as strong as the benefits they want to achieve.

Complete the table below in relation to the change you specified above, listing on one side the benefits of making that change in behavior and on the other side all the potential drawbacks you feel there may be.

Benefits	Drawbacks

Dealing With Drawbacks

Specify any things that you can do or say to yourself to help manage or deal with any of the drawbacks you listed above:

_____

_____

_____

_____

_____

_____

Action (Massive Action)

Now specify what you are going to try out considering your previous answers to try to improve your relationship. Remember, this exercise can be for any type of relationship. Indicate:

- *How you are going to try to act or change your approach*

_____

_____

- *When you are going to do it*

_____

_____

_____

- *How you are going to assess whether it is working*

_____

_____

_____

_____

- *Whether you are going to tell the other person in the relationship beforehand what you are going to try to do*

_____

_____

_____

_____

- *Whether you're going to seek feedback (afterward) from the other person in the relationship on what you try*

_____

_____

_____

- ***Any support you are going to seek (and from whom)***

_____

_____

_____

Loving And Assertive Communication

Loving and assertive communication involves expressing your thoughts, needs, and boundaries while maintaining respect, empathy, and care for the other person. Here are a few examples of loving and assertive communication:

1. "I feel hurt when you cancel our plans without letting me know in advance. It's important to me that we communicate and respect each other's time. Can we find a way to address this issue?"

2. "I appreciate that you're trying to help, but I would prefer if you asked for my consent before offering advice. I value your input, but I also want to have the freedom to make my own decisions."

3. "I understand that you're frustrated, but yelling and insults don't resolve the issue. Let's take a moment to calm down and discuss this problem calmly and respectfully. I believe we can find a solution together."

4. "I love spending time with you, and it's important to me that we have equal opportunities to pursue our individual interests. Can we create a schedule that allows both of us to engage in our hobbies while still making time for each other?"

5. "When you interrupt me during conversations, I feel like my opinions are not valued. It would mean a lot to me if you could allow me to finish speaking before sharing your thoughts. That way, we can have a more productive and respectful conversation."

6. "I understand that you may have different expectations, but I need to be honest about my own needs. I need some space and alone time to recharge. It doesn't mean I don't care about you, it's just how I function."

Remember, loving and assertive communication involves expressing yourself honestly and directly while considering the feelings and perspectives of others. It's about finding a balance between being true to yourself and fostering healthy and respectful relationships.

In my training and professional experience, I have come across many tools, strategies, and interventions for various concerns. The following communication framework is simple yet effective in keeping the communication clear and assertive.

The DEAL Method is an approach people can try when they find they have difficulty voicing their needs to others and explaining clearly and calmly to others how they would like others to act (or not act) towards them. The acronym **DEAL** stands for:

Describe the situation or behavior that is a concern for you

Express your feelings and thoughts about it

Ask for reasonable changes that you feel would help

Listen & Negotiate for a reasonable solution if possible

To help you see how to use the **DEAL** method, here's an example: Let's assume that you feel exhausted and resentful because you are doing all the childcare and housework in your household and you would like your partner to help out, but you are afraid of the reaction if you bring it up. You might approach it by going through the steps above and preparing what you would say in advance. When discussing difficult situations, keep in mind that you have space to talk about it as opposed to a time that's pressured. I believe that it's wise to always take a few deep breaths before a charged conversation as it can help regulate the nervous emotions you may have going in. Know that during the conversation, pausing and taking deep deliberate breaths will help keep you calm, and if you get overly dysregulated, pause, walk away, take a break, take your deep breaths during the break, and resume when you are calm.

- **DESCRIBE** the situation

In describing the situation, it helps to be clear and specific, giving an example of the problem, describing the action/behavior, refraining from attacking, using generalized language, or getting all up in your feelings. For example, instead of saying, "Why don't you ever help me with the kids?!" which most likely will be met with some resistance. Another way to say it is, "I've been thinking about the arrangements for Saturday night, and I realized that it may create a problem for me to watch them that night. I was hoping to go out with my friend because it's her birthday and it won't be possible if I have to stay at home with the kids."

- **EXPRESS** Your feelings and thoughts about it.

Feelings and thoughts are yours until you share them. It may seem obvious to you, but the other person may not necessarily know. Try your best to explain to them how the situation/behavior is making you feel. You might say this: "I feel hurt that you haven't offered to help out in this situation and that I am doing most of the household chores and childcare which is leaving me tired. For example, last week it was me who put the kids to bed, made dinner, and cleaned the kitchen after meals every day. After coming home after a long day at work it's really tiring for me."

Remember, you want to use comfortable language in your style and vocabulary while following the key principles:

> *AVOID extreme or overly emotional language*

> *KEEP the statement simple and accurate*

> *EXPRESS your feelings and indicate what is the basis for them*

> ➤ *OWN* feelings as your own - you are acknowledging that this is how you feel, not suggesting that everyone would necessarily feel that way

- **ASK** for reasonable changes that you feel would help

Remember people aren't mind readers so being specific is key. For example, "Would it be possible for you to look after the kids on Saturday night so I can go out? I can watch them on Friday if you want to go out then. I wonder if we could also talk in advance about the options for sharing responsibilities next week and see if we can agree on arrangements that give us both the opportunity to have some time for ourselves."

When asking for changes, it is again important to be clear and direct about what it is you are asking while being polite and not over-personalizing the request with emotive critical descriptions of the other person. If there are examples when the other person has done what you would like them to do, then one possibility is to start by focusing on these. For example, "On Thursday, it really helped when you watched the kids for a couple of hours. If you can do a similar thing again, I would appreciate it."

In the interests of reasonableness and balance, if appropriate, make clear that you are not saying the other person is all bad by highlighting positives as well as being clear about what you would like them to do differently and why.

- **LISTEN & NEGOTIATE** a reasonable solution where possible

In most cases, the other person may have a different perspective on the situation. If you haven't expressed your concerns before or if you expressed it in a way that was not assertive, they may not even be aware of your feelings.

Alternatively, there may be reasons and thoughts behind their behavior and actions that you have not considered. For example, the partner in the example I used may feel that there are a lot of tasks that they do, that you don't help out with.

Once you have expressed your thoughts and feelings and what you would like, it is therefore important to check out what the other person thinks. You can ask, "What do you think? Or "What are your thoughts about it?" Once the other person has responded, and if they are not fully in agreement with what you have suggested, then you can try to explore with them whether an alternative solution is possible. This will involve considering:

(a) What is most important to you in this situation and what is most important to them? Is it possible to meet both your priorities?

(b) What alternatives are possible? Could you get a babysitter for the specific instances above and then agree to future arrangements?

(c) In what ways are you both willing to compromise?

(d) If a compromise cannot be reached, then what are the implications for the relationship and what choices do you have for the future?

(e) If an agreement is reached, then confirm exactly what it is and clarify any gray areas. In a formal situation, you may also want to make a written note of it and share that with the other person if appropriate.

EXERCISE

Time to get into MASSIVE ACTION! Using the DEAL Method, make your own notes under each step of how the method applies to a situation you are concerned about where you are having difficulty expressing your needs, or where you would like someone to change their behavior towards you. For each step, note what you propose to say and do in relation to that step when you speak to the person concerned.

Describe the situation or behavior that is a concern for you

_____

_____

_____

_____

_____

Express your feelings and thoughts about it

_____

_____

_____

_____

_____

Ask for reasonable changes that you feel would help

_____

_____

_____

_____

_____

Listen & Negotiate for a reasonable solution if possible

_____

_____

_____

_____

I wasn't familiar with this technique and didn't know this was happening when I made a request. I didn't quite get what I wanted but I did get a solution to the problem. Many years ago, and fairly early in my second marriage, I found myself getting frustrated and feeling burned out because I worked full-time and did all the housework. I was at my tipping point after I read *Lean In: Women, Work, and the Will to Lead*, a book encouraging women to assert themselves at work and at home, by business executive Sheryl Sandberg. The book inspired me to express my concerns with my ex-husband and my need for help. Unfortunately, he did not bend but doubled down and recommended I get a maid and that was exactly what I did. I got someone to come every two weeks. Did I want him to contribute to the household duties? Yes, but at the end of the day, I did get some relief with the paid assistance and that was the real problem I wanted solved. I got some relief.

Learn The Power Of 'No', Setting Boundaries, and Speaking Up

One of the most challenging things many of us need to learn in order to be happy and enjoy life more is the ability to set boundaries - both with others and ourselves. A boundary is when we draw a line in the sand recognizing what we need - and ensuring we get that need met. It is about taking care of ourselves. Often this involves saying "NO" to others or ourselves. But it can also mean standing up for ourselves, speaking out, and defining what we will and will not accept with respect to how we are treated.

As women, we can have poor boundaries for a variety of reasons, including socialization, internalization, sexism, and the inherent pressure to be accommodating. Historically, women have been expected to be subservient and to prioritize the needs of others. This often leads to women disregarding their own wants and needs, and we end up feeling guilty for setting boundaries and not feeling comfortable saying no. We also are taught from a young age that expressing anger and other strong emotions is inappropriate, which can make it difficult for us to assert boundaries. Additionally, the prevalence of sexism, misogyny, and other harmful societal messages can make it even harder for women to communicate their boundaries clearly and directly.

Boundaries are one thing my clients have said they struggle with most within relationships. I too have had loose boundaries in my relationships, and it has caused me much grief. Yet I have learned through trial and tribulations so that you don't have to. Do you find it hard to say no? If this has been an area of concern in the past, look no further. You are about to get your whole "personal space" back.

Setting Healthy Personal Boundaries

What is a boundary?

Clearly defined limits within which you are free to be yourself with no restrictions placed on you by others as to how to think, feel, or act.

Why are boundaries so darn hard for people?

1. Fear of conflict. People may avoid setting boundaries because they fear confrontation or negative reactions from others. They may worry about hurting someone's feelings, damaging relationships, or being perceived as selfish or rude. This fear of conflict can lead to people ignoring or sacrificing their own needs, which can be detrimental to their well-being.

2. Desire for approval. People naturally seek acceptance and approval from others. They may prioritize maintaining harmonious relationships over asserting their own boundaries. The fear of disappointing or displeasing others can make it challenging to set and communicate boundaries effectively. People pleasing is one of the main behaviors my clients struggle with.

3. Low self-esteem. Individuals with low self-esteem may not feel deserving of having their boundaries respected. They may struggle with asserting themselves or feel guilty for prioritizing their own needs. This lack of self-worth can make it difficult to establish and maintain healthy boundaries.

4. Lack of awareness. Some people may not even be aware of their own needs, desires, or limits. They may be disconnected from their emotions or have a habit of putting others' needs before their own. Without self-awareness, it becomes challenging to identify and communicate personal boundaries effectively.

5. Cultural and societal influences. Cultural and societal norms can also play a role in making boundary-setting difficult. Some cultures prioritize collectivism and interdependence, where individual needs may be subordinated to the needs of the group or family. Additionally, societal messages about being accommodating, selfless, or always available can create a barrier to setting personal boundaries.

6. Past experiences. Negative past experiences, such as boundary violations, abuse, or trauma, can make it harder for individuals to establish boundaries. They may have a heightened fear of being vulnerable or trust issues that make it challenging to set and enforce boundaries in future relationships.

Eight Basic Principles of Healthy Boundary Setting

1. *Establishing boundaries makes you a safe person.* People know where they stand with you. Boundaries are the way we take care of ourselves. We have both a right and a duty to protect and defend ourselves.

2. *Generous people set boundaries.* If you don't set boundaries, you are giving yourself away. With boundaries, you only give what you want, which means you can afford to be generous to more people over a longer period of time. Remember we are only giving from our overflow.

3. *Boundaries allow others to grow.* This makes others conscious of their behavior, thus allowing

them to change.

4.   *Boundaries allow you to get more of what you want, and less of what you don't.* Boundaries not only protect you from unwanted behavior, but they also foster the behavior that you want.

5.   *Effective people set boundaries.* Doing so keeps you in control of your time and efforts, which makes you feel better about yourself. This leads to your being more effective.

6.   *Stick to your guns.* In order for boundary settings to work for you, you must develop a commitment to uphold what is right and true for you. You must act consistently in upholding your boundaries.

7.   *Practice makes perfect.* If this is not familiar behavior it will feel awkward and unnatural at first, but anything worth doing is worth doing badly at first. People may not like it at first, but that's natural; they are used to getting their own way with you. Trust me, they will adapt, because people adjust.

8.   *Keep it up.* With practice, you will become more skillful and graceful. Uphold the boundary unapologetically.

Guidelines for Setting Effective Boundaries

- Back up boundary setting with action.
- Be direct, firm, and gracious.
- Don't debate, defend or over-explain.
- Have support easily available on the sidelines in the beginning.
- Stay strong, don't give in.

Situational Examples of Setting Healthy Boundaries

- *Anger* - "You may not continue to yell at me. If you do, I will leave the room and end this meeting."

- *Buy Time* - "I have a policy of not making snap decisions. I need time to think and reflect on what I want to do. If you need an immediate answer, it will be no."

- *Criticism* - "It's not okay with me for you to make comments about my weight. Please stop. If you don't, I won't be able to continue this conversation."

- *Extra Commitments* - "Although this is an important issue to me, I must decline your request for my help at this time." Or "I need to honor my family's needs."

- *Money* - "I won't be lending you any more money. I care about you, and you need to start taking responsibility for yourself."

REMEMBER, it is not enough to set boundaries. It is necessary to be willing to do whatever it takes to enforce them. Enforcing boundaries means following through with consequences.

Guidelines for Setting Consequences

- Set forth clearly and unemotionally.
- Actions you are willing to take.
- May allow for gradual change.
- May be negotiable rather than rigid lines in the sand.

Examples of Stating Clear Consequences

- "If you break plans with me by not showing up or calling me, I will call you out on your behavior and let you know how I feel."

- "If you continue (offensive behavior) I will leave the room/house/ ask you to leave."

- "If you continue to repeat the behavior, I will consider all of my options including leaving the relationship."

- "If you continue to ignore my solutions or suggestions, I will assume that you are not interested in receiving help from me and I will stop working on your case."

If you are not ready to end a relationship or conversation, don't say you are until you really are. If people are unwilling to respect your boundaries, they are not true friends or people you want to spend time with. Setting personal boundaries and limits can be very important in how you lead your life and the quality of the relationships you have.

How to Establish Healthier Boundaries

Follow these steps to effectively establish healthy boundaries between yourself and others.

First: Identify the symptoms of your boundaries currently being or having been violated or ignored.

Second: Identify the irrational or unhealthy thinking and beliefs by which you allow your boundaries to be ignored or violated.

Third: Identify new, more rational, healthy thinking and beliefs that will encourage you to change your behaviors so that you build healthy boundaries between yourself and others.

Fourth: Identify new behaviors you need to add to your healthy boundary-building behaviors repertoire to sustain healthy boundaries between you and others.

Fifth: Implement healthy boundary-building beliefs and behaviors in your life so that your space, privacy, and rights are no longer ignored or violated.

Who do you most need to set boundaries with? (make a list)

_____

_____

_____

_____

_____

Where do you need to set boundaries with yourself?

_____

_____

_____

_____

_____

Ask yourself, "If I say 'yes' to that, what I will be saying 'no' to?

_____

_____

_____

_____

_____

Then, if I say 'no', what will I be saying 'yes' to?

_____

_____

_____

What is the biggest thing that stops you from setting and maintaining boundaries?

_____

_____

_____

_____

_____

Choose you! What three boundaries can be set to ensure your needs are being met?

1. _____

2. _____

3. _____

Steps to Improve or Remove

Loving and being loved is a wonderful feeling. Unfortunately, as much as we want a situation to work, there may come a time when you will have to decide to leave a relationship that is not honoring you and meeting your needs. Before you decide to remove yourself, be intentional with your effort to improve the situation. That may require you to get some support and go to therapy. That may require you to go to drug or alcohol treatment. That might require you to get serious about your health. Whatever it is, deal with your 'ish' first. Deal with your unresolved hurts, grief, and loss. You can only improve and heal yourself.

Use the table below to list the things you like about a particular relationship and the good feelings generated by them as well as the things you dislike about the relationship and the negative feelings generated.

Positive Aspects of the Relationship	Feelings Generated by The Positive Aspects	Negative Aspects of The Relationship	Feelings Generated by The Negative Aspects

Look at the *feelings* generated by the negative aspects. What could you do to reduce the negative impact of those feelings? This might involve either or both of:

(a) *Finding a way of changing the thing that has given rise to the feeling.*

•

•

•

OR

(b) *Finding a way of reacting differently to it.*

•

•

•

Ending A Relationship

In my last marriage, I felt a deep connection to my ex-husband. We grew from a friendship. Early on, we laughed with each other. We spent a lot of time with each other. We were foodies and we loved to go out to eat. We had similar tastes in music and art, and we agreed on some viewpoints, although I was way more of a humanitarian and was idealistic. I reflect on when things shifted to the point of no return. He held a grudge from when I hooked up with someone else when we were dating and threw it in my face, repeatedly, for over a decade and I quietly resented him for having a two-year affair when we first got married. We both felt betrayed and subconsciously it showed. We tried therapy many times. In the end, we had a husband-and-wife therapist duo team from Atlanta, GA, known as *That Clay Couple.* Even with their wisdom and counsel, we just could not get on the same page.

In 2022, I had to write a new chapter for myself called *I Choose Me, Unapologetically.* It's not easy to walk away from a person that you once loved. It takes courage. I didn't realize when I named my business seven years ago, Empowered by Courage, that I would have to make decisions that took courage, by which I am immensely empowered by.

What might you say to your partner to make the break? *(if you can think of more than one option, then write down each option before deciding which one to use. Analyze the advantages and disadvantages of each)*	When and where might you say it?	How best can you act to inform your partner of the breakup to stick to your decision?

Sometimes people are reluctant to leave because of their attachment to the person. Have you ever had to choose yourself and walk away from a situation that no longer was for you? Was it hard? Do you have any regrets?

This exercise is for people who have definitively decided to end a relationship but are having difficulty carrying it through. This allows you to write down what you are going to do. The table applies to a relationship with a partner, but you could also use it for other relationships.

Ending a relationship can be a difficult and emotional process. If you're having trouble carrying it through, here are some guidelines that may help you navigate the situation:

1. *Reflect on your decision.* Before taking any action, make sure you're certain about ending the relationship. Consider your reasons, the impact it will have on both of you, and whether you've exhausted all possible solutions.

2. *Choose an appropriate time and place.* Find a suitable environment where you can have an open and honest conversation without interruptions. Avoid public places or times when your partner may be preoccupied or stressed.

3. *Be honest and respectful.* When communicating your decision, be honest but compassionate. Clearly express your feelings and reasons for ending the relationship while avoiding blame or criticism. Use "I" statements to express how you feel, rather than making sweeping generalizations about your partner.

4. *Listen actively.* Allow your partner to express their thoughts and emotions without

interruption. It's important to show empathy and validate their feelings, even if you don't agree with everything they say.

5. *Provide closure and answer questions.* Ending a relationship can leave the other person with many questions. While it's essential to maintain your boundaries, try to address their concerns and provide some closure. However, avoid giving false hope or making promises you can't keep.

6. *Establish and maintain boundaries.* After the breakup, it's crucial to establish clear boundaries to allow both of you to heal and move on. Communicate your expectations regarding contact, social media, and shared spaces, and respect each other's need for space and time apart.

7. *Seek support.* Ending a relationship can be emotionally challenging, so it's important to lean on your support system. Share your feelings and concerns with trusted friends or family members who can provide guidance and understanding.

8. *Take care of yourself.* Focus on self-care. Engage in activities that bring you joy, practice self-compassion, and consider seeking professional help if you're struggling with the emotional aftermath of the breakup.

Remember, ending a relationship is rarely easy, but sometimes it's necessary for personal growth and happiness. Be patient with yourself and allow both you and that person the time and space to heal.

The Most Important Relationship Is with *Yourself*

In my humble opinion based on my experiences and observations, the greatest, sweetest, and most satisfying relationship you can ever have is with yourself. *You* are the key. You are love. You are enough. Your love for yourself is an endless gift to you. We at times will put other's needs ahead of ours, leaving us suffering. Take your power back and love on yourself. Protect your peace. Be assured that when you establish a good relationship with yourself, you are cultivating yourself through self-care and self-esteem, which is an important aspect of personal growth and overall well-being.

When you have a healthy sense of self and self-love, there will be people, places, and things you will find are not in alignment with your greater sense of well-being. You will be empowered to make choices that are for your higher good. Sis, this is the radical act of choosing *you*, unapologetically. As a reminder, the most important highlights of honing *The Art of Choosing You Unapologetically* are:

1. ***Practice self-acceptance.*** Embrace yourself as you are, with all your strengths and weaknesses. Recognize that nobody is perfect, and it's okay to have flaws and make mistakes. Treat yourself with kindness, compassion, and forgiveness.

2. ***Prioritize self-care***. Take care of your physical, mental, and emotional well-being. Engage in activities that bring you joy, relaxation, and fulfillment. Make time for hobbies, exercise regularly, eat nutritious food, get enough sleep, and practice stress management techniques such as meditation or deep breathing exercises.

3. ***Set healthy boundaries.*** Identify and communicate your needs, desires, and limits to others. Learn to say "no" when necessary and create space for yourself. Respecting your own boundaries helps you maintain a sense of self-worth and prevents burnout.

4. ***Practice positive self-talk.*** Be mindful of your internal dialogue and challenge negative thoughts or self-criticism. Replace self-doubt and self-judgment with positive affirmations. Focus on your strengths, achievements, and qualities. Surround yourself with supportive and encouraging people who uplift you.

5. ***Engage in self-reflection.*** Take time to understand yourself better. Reflect on your values,

beliefs, goals, and desires. Journaling, meditation, or seeking therapy can help you gain clarity and insight into your thoughts and emotions.

6. ***Cultivate self-compassion.*** Treat yourself with the same kindness and understanding you would offer to a close friend. Acknowledge your mistakes and setbacks without harsh self-judgment. Practice self-compassion by embracing your humanness and giving yourself permission to learn and grow.

7. ***Invest in personal growth.*** Engage in activities that promote personal development and expand your knowledge and skills. Set realistic goals and work towards them, as progress and achievement can boost self-confidence and self-esteem.

8. ***Surround yourself with positive influences.*** Surround yourself with people who support and inspire you. Consider working with a life coach for support and guidance. Build relationships with individuals who value and respect you for who you are. Minimize contact with toxic or negative individuals who drain your energy or bring you down.

Remember that building a healthy relationship with yourself is an ongoing process that requires patience, self-reflection, and self-care. Be consistent in practicing these habits, and over time you will see improvements in your self-esteem and overall well-being.

In closing, having the ability to live a life full with no regrets requires us to be fearless in our pursuits to inspire us and be vigilant in caring for ourselves on a deeper level. Remember it starts with *you* and the love for yourself. I hope that the EMPOWER framework spoke to your heart and you were touched, moved, and inspired to give yourself the permission to be guiltless and become the master of the art of choosing you, unapologetically.

About the Author

Renee Cage is a licensed mental health therapist, life coach, and international speaker who has dedicated her life's work to community empowerment, restorative justice, and advocacy. Born and raised in Oakland, CA, Renee considers herself a "rose from the concrete" and has used her experiences as a survivor of childhood trauma to fuel her passion for supporting others. With over 30 years of experience in social work, mental health, and leadership, Renee founded Empowered by Courage, LLC, a counseling, coaching, and consulting firm dedicated to transforming individuals and corporations to achieve success on their terms.

Renee has a unique gift for empowering professional women who look like they have it all, but they're stressed out and silently screaming inside, "Is this it?" Rewind several years, that was Renee. Her physical and mental health was deteriorating. She hit a wall in her career, self-doubt ate at her and life just felt overwhelming. She knew something had to give.

She learned how she was creating her misery with her mindset and how that played a major role in how she viewed her circumstances, how she managed her time, and ultimately her life. Renee went from waking up exhausted and worried about how to get everything done to waking up ahead of the game, full of energy, and in control of her time while living out her purpose.

That's why she created the E.M.P.O.W.E.R. Mindset Formula and began teaching ambitious women how they can do the same. Renee's dedication to empowering women has inspired her to create various programs and courses including Uncover Your Procrastination Style & Eradicate It, and Exhausted to Empowered program. Her latest book, *The Art of Choosing Yourself Unapologetically, 8 Steps to Happiness, Health, and Wellness* is a testament to her commitment to inspiring women to prioritize themselves and reject the pressure to be Superwoman.